PRACTICAL
SOLUTIONS
TO EVERYDAY PROBLEMS

PRACTICAL SOLUTIONS

TO EVERYDAY PROBLEMS

*Achieve Inner Peace
and Optimal Performance*

Neil A. Fiore, Ph.D.

MEDIA

Published 2021 by Gildan Media LLC
aka G&D Media
www.GandDmedia.com

First Edition: 2021

Front cover design by David Rheinhardt of Pyrographx

Interior design by Meghan Day Healey of Story Horse, LLC.

Library of Congress Cataloging-in-Publication Data is available upon request

ISBN: 978-1-7225-0550-9

10   9   8   7   6   5   4   3   2   1

Contents

Part I
Practical Solutions

Part II
Beyond Practical Solutions
Digging Deeper

To the Reader

Practical Solutions to Everyday Problems gives you not just a sample but the essence of applying strategic, solution-focused therapy to resolving what I call "normal problems." It is my hope that it will set you free of erroneous concepts, feelings, and beliefs about yourself that may be keeping you from experiencing the full joy of your unique version of life. In these pages you could find a new perspective on how to live your life free of excessive anxiety, stress, and worry. You could discover how to tap deeper resources within yourself that have been repressed by early training and fear. It is my hope that this book will help you warm to life those aspects of your true self that you had to freeze away in order to fit in or to just survive.

Acknowledgments

This book is the result of over forty years of work as a clinical psychologist with clients and as a coach to entrepreneurs and CEOS—and from work on myself—to discover clear and practical paths to inner peace and optimal performance. This book is dedicated to my coaching and therapy clients who have motivated me to provide practical solutions to problems for which they have courageously sought help.

Writing *Practical Solutions to Everyday Problems* would have taken longer and been more difficult and less enjoyable without the support, advice, and encouragement of Diana Marie Nugent, Penny Washbourn, and Marika Kuzma.

Practical Solutions to Everyday Problems also results from my study of the writings and examples given by many notable thinkers and authors, several of whom I've had the good fortunate to study with directly. I recommend their books to you if you wish to read the primary sources from which I've drawn many of the concepts and exercises contained in this book. They include: Roberto Assagioli, Sylvia Boorstein, Joan Borysenko, Joseph Campbell, Mihaly Csikszentmihalyi, the Dalai Lama, Ram Dass, Pierre Teilhard de Chardin, Anthony de Mello, Wayne Dyer, Karlfried Durckheim, Milton H. Erickson, Matthew Fox, Erich Fromm, Tim Gallwey, Kabir Edmund Helminski, Jean Houston, Louise Kaplan, Harold Kushner, Thich Nhat Hanh, Carl Jung, Jack Kornfield, George Leonard, Stephen Levine, Donald Meichenbaum, Dan Millman, Wayne Muller, Michael Murphy, Wendy Palmer, Fritz Perls, H. W. L. Poonja, John C. Robinson, David Richo, Ernest Rossi, Martin Seligman, Herbert and David Spiegel, Charles Spielberger, Richard Suinn, D. T. Suzuki, Shunryu Suzuki, John and Helen Watkins, Alan Watts, John Welwood, Ken Wilber, and Colin Wilson.

Introduction

Everything can be taken from a man but one thing:
the last of human freedoms—to choose one's attitude in any given set of circumstances, to choose
one's own way.

—VIKTOR E. FRANKL, *Man's Search for Meaning*

This book is based on my work as a psychologist and
coach applying solutions-focused therapy, cognitive
behavioral therapy (CBT), dialectic behavioral therapy
(DBT), and clinical hypnosis to help clients with relatively normal problems to live productive and joyful
lives. *Practical Solutions* offers tools for living a satisfy-
ing life through self-mastery and self-leadership.

This book is not psychoanalysis, nor is it a substitute
for individual therapy; it is the application of common

sense and strategic psychology to the creative resolution of problems that routinely keep many of us stuck. As opposed to the all too frequent "Why did you spill the milk?", this pragmatic approach asks, "How can you clean it up?" Instead of assuming that the one spilling the milk has some hidden motive or has something wrong with them, the approach offered here focuses attention on fixing the problem and dealing with the task at hand. It is based on the belief that to be optimally effective and productive, we need to focus on the task, not judge the individual.

This work is based on my experience as a licensed psychologist at the Counseling Center at the University of California, Berkeley, and in private practice; as the author of six books; and as an international speaker who has given hundreds of workshops and presentations around the world (including at the Smithsonian Institution, the Commonwealth Club, Esalen Institute, Kaiser hospitals, the University of California at San Francisco, Stanford University, and St. Peter's University). But a more compelling reason to read and apply the strategies and tools of *Practical Solutions to Everyday Problems* may be what I learned as a survivor: of what was diagnosed as terminal cancer at the age of thirty-two; and as a survivor of the war in Vietnam while serving with the 101st Airborne Division. These experiences rapidly transformed my life and sparked my passion to discover how to help others make rapid changes without suffering through cancer, war, or years of therapy.

Facing a life-threatening diagnosis replaces arrogance with a more realistic humility for our human vulnerability and replaces fear with the knowledge that once we have faced the worst, there is nothing more to fear but inaction. Join me in taking positive steps toward a fuller life by identifying and addressing the major issues that may be keeping you from fully enjoying and celebrating your life.

Practical Solutions outlines the most frequent issues that clients present in my office. To each of these issues I have given suggestions called "Practical Solution," "Imagery," "Putting It to Use," and "Hot Tip."

Objectives

1. Readers will learn how their self-talk can cause either inner peace or stress and anxiety.
2. Readers will achieve greater control over their issues by applying the exercises and strategies.
3. Readers will acquire an understanding of how to play a leadership role in their lives and how to more effectively manage challenges and common problems.
4. Readers will achieve an enhanced sense of self along with greater confidence and self-esteem.
5. Readers will learn how to gain control over negative habits and replace them with productive habits.

Five Signs That You Can Benefit from This Book

At least five major symptoms and problem areas are reduced or resolved by applying the practical solutions process. They are: stress and fear; inner conflict and procrastination; self-criticism and self-doubt; feeling overwhelmed; and unnecessary struggle and frustration.

Within just a few chapters, you'll be shifting your identity away from your symptoms and default reactions into the role and voice of your leadership Self. From a new perspective, you'll minimize or completely remove many of the blocks that have kept you from realizing your true potential for happiness, success, and inner peace.

Notice how many of the following symptoms describe your current behavior and negative internal dialogue. Identify the symptoms in yourself without self-criticism, but with an appreciation that you've taken the first step to freeing yourself of old, destructive patterns.

1. **Stress, fear, anxiety, or worry (lacking safety and worth). Symptoms:**
   - You frequently are afraid that something awful will happen and cause you to be angry with yourself.
   - Your ego and self-worth are always on the line—available to be judged by others—at work, in leisure activities, and in your relationships.
   - You try to cope with anxiety by relying on a variety of addictive habits or crutches—such as over-indulging in coffee, sweets, alcohol, or becoming dependent in your relationships.
   - You attempt to control others and events in the hope of avoiding threats to your self-worth and to avoid disappointment.
   - You often find it difficult to sleep because your mind is racing with worries and anxiety.

Negative self-talk: "What if something goes wrong? What if they don't like it? I couldn't stand it if I fail. I lack confidence and am afraid of what others think about my appearance, my work, and me. If I suffer another loss, I'll feel miserable and worthless."

2. Inner conflict, indecisiveness, procrastination (lacking a sense of choice). Symptoms:

- ❧ You work hard, but your fear of making a mistake and being criticized causes you to procrastinate and be indecisive.
- ❧ You use threats and criticism to try to motivate yourself, but it only makes things worse.
- ❧ You tell yourself, *"You have to do it,"* but then feel, *"I don't want to"*—causing inner conflict that stalls your progress and sabotages the achievement of your goals
- ❧ You delay calling your family and friends or clients and customers because you feel guilty and ashamed about procrastinating on your commitments to them.
- ❧ You resent anyone in authority—a parent, teacher, or boss—and resist doing any work you don't want to do, causing you to be late or to turn in substandard work at the last minute.

Negative self-talk: "I should, but I don't want to. I have to finish a very important project, must do it perfectly, and must endure a life with no fun. I don't want to have to do this. I have no choice. I work best under pressure. I just want to get this over with."

3. Self-criticism and self-blame (lacking self-acceptance and task-oriented focus). Symptoms:

- ☙ You believe that a part of you is weak and needs criticism, threats, and constant nagging.
- ☙ You feel that whatever you do is never good enough for others or yourself, and you should have started earlier.
- ☙ You seldom accept yourself, and if you do, it's only when your performance is exceptional and nearly impossible to repeat.
- ☙ You feel that some part of you makes things difficult and sabotages your success.
- ☙ You focus on what's wrong with you—"Why did you spill the milk?"—rather than on what it takes just to do the job: "How can we clean it up? When do we start?"

Negative self-talk: "Why can't I do this? What's wrong with me? You should be stronger and try harder. You should have started earlier; you're such a procrastinator. You'll never succeed at this rate? I hate my life."

4. Being overwhelmed with projects and goals (lacking peace in the present moment). Symptoms:

- ❦ You try to do it all and don't know when to ask for help or to acknowledge that the workload and personal responsibilities are too much for you.

- ❦ You spend an inordinate amount of time trying to maximize your possibilities and then try to control people and events in a desperate attempt to succeed.

- ❦ You have a smorgasbord approach to life—buying every new gadget and fad—with a tendency to gobble lots of objects, food, and people rather than savoring a few.

- ❦ You find it difficult to stay focused on one project. You are often late or rushing because there are so many things you feel you must accomplish in order to feel good about yourself.

- ❦ You repeatedly overschedule your day and feel trapped, with too many tasks and obligations.

Negative self-talk: "I have to finish it all. I don't know where to start. I want to do it all, but there's too much to do. I'm overwhelmed, burnt out, and exhausted."

5. Struggling from a limited identity (lacking connection with a larger, leadership Self). Symptoms:

- ❧ You feel you must do everything on your own; there's no one else to support you; no one you can trust to do it as well as you.

- ❧ You're desperately searching and striving for peace, joy, and fulfillment in something or someone, but can't seem to find it.

- ❧ You feel exhausted and burnt out, so you try to escape by watching TV, overeating, surfing the Internet, texting, or talking on the phone.

- ❧ You work long hours, seldom relax, binge on junk food, alcohol, cigarettes, and distractions, but seldom feel renewed or satisfied.

- ❧ You remind yourself to be tough—"I don't need anybody"—but at times you wish you could trust someone to help you.

Negative self-talk: "I have to try harder, but I feel burnt out. I'm tired of working so hard and getting nowhere. But I can't see any other way except to just keep trying to get by, propping myself up with whatever drug or distraction is available."

*   *   *

Scoring: If you recognize yourself in all of the symptoms associated with one problem area or more than fifteen of the twenty-five total symptoms, then you definitely could benefit from reading this book. By first identifying your symptoms and negative inner dialogue, you're preparing to transform your life by shifting to your higher, leadership Self and the five qualities (worth, choice, self-acceptance, inner peace, connection to your leadership Self) that replace those symptoms. Better still, you can start today to apply practical solutions to enhance your life by expanding your sense of self to include more of your brain and its self-leadership roles and deeper resources.

Part I
Practical Solutions

Anxiety

Anxiety is often confused with stress, but they are very different. You evoke anxiety when you think about an event in the imaginary past or future and your body tries to get there, leaving you stuck with energy you can't use now. Stress is a survival response that provides adrenalin and other corticosteroids to prepare you for fight or flight when there's a threat to your physical safety.

Practical solution.

Bring your mind into the present; be mindful of your breathing and your physical feelings. Wake up all your senses in this moment—the sounds, smells, and sensations. There is no anxiety when your mind is in the present with your body.

Exercise.

Notice what's around you and complete these statements:

Now I'm aware of this sound.

_____

Now I'm aware of this sensation.

_____

Now I'm aware of this smell.

_____

Now I'm aware of this view/image.

_____

This exercise will help you connect to your body, to the earth, the building, the floor, the chair. Accept the support of the laws of nature. Notice how you feel connected to a larger system of support. You are no longer struggling as if alone. This is the power of mindfulness and of Ram Dass's famous instruction: *be here now.* You'll become more fully alive in this moment—the only moment there is. Bring your time traveling mind back from the imaginary past and future into the real present with your body.

Imagery.

Imagine that your body is trying to follow your mind through a wall into the future problem. But it can't get into an imaginary time. Think of anxiety as stuck energy that cannot be used now. There is only now!

The past and the future are imaginary. Your body is grounded in the only time that is real: the present.

When you bring your awareness back into the present, your energy is unstuck and can be used effectively. You are free of the paralysis caused by anxiety's stuck energy.

Ask yourself: "What can I do *now*? What can I do now to prepare for that imagined future problem?" Use the unstuck energy of released anxiety to motivate yourself to plan and problem-solve.

Thinking about a future problem can be helpful only when you start a plan in the present. You can only achieve your future goal by starting now, in the present.

Putting it to use.

When you start to feel anxious, notice the time frame (usually future or past) that you're imagining. Bring your mind into the present sensations of your body, grounding yourself into the chair, the floor, the earth, or the playing field. Exhale images of the past or future and float down into the present and the support of the laws of nature.

Hot tip.

Inhale, hold your breath, tense your muscles for five seconds, then exhale and release muscle tension. As your body floats down into the present, bring your mind into your body's present sensations, out of the imaginary past or future. Your mind is now with your body in the present, where you can take positive action to prepare for any real or imagined future problem.

Stress

Practical solution.

Make yourself safe with *you*. Stress is a survival response triggered by signals of danger—an earthquake, a tornado, a gunshot—that is, real threats to your life. If you're physically safe in your office and you experience a stress response because of an email, text, or a telephone call, it is your thinking and self-talk that have evoked the survival response. Your mind interpreted those relatively mild events as a serious threat to your safety and peace. Decide if you really need an adrenaline-fueled survival response to cope with a criticism, rejection, or a poor evaluation.

When you decide it's safe to exhale and release muscle tension, you shut off the stress/survival alarm. Remarkably, your reptilian (fight-or-flight) reaction will shut off when your higher, human brain gives the all clear signal—for example, "This is only a 3.0 earth-quake; it's safe to return to a normal level of alertness. We're safe. I don't need the stress of fight-or-flight response."

Imagery.

Imagine how you will make yourself feel today: happy, stressed, anxious, sad? Unless you're in a situation of life-threatening danger—in which the stress/survival response is appropriate—your experience of stress is coming from threatening yourself with messages such as: "I will make you feel miserable and worthless if this happens and I don't get what I want." To lower stress, stop threatening yourself. Guarantee your safety regardless of what happens or what others say. Know that you will not abandon yourself if something negative happens; promise that you will not give up on your unique version of life.

When you experience a stress response, notice if it's triggered by an external event or what you're saying to yourself. If no one is shooting at you and there are no natural disasters occurring, you most likely are threatening yourself. Something as common as "I *have to* finish all this work" can trigger a stress response by suggesting that something awful will happen if you fail to complete everything on time. *Have to* implies that you don't want to; they're making you do something against your will; you should rebel. It also implies a threat, as in, "You *have to, or else* I will punish you with something dreadful."

The main causes of stress are probably some form of self-hatred or self-criticism coming from within yourself.

Calling up the stress response to deal with dangers that are not happening now is similar to pulling a fire alarm for a fire that happened twenty years ago or to fearing a fire that may happen next year. It would be unfair to the fire department and a misuse of its time and energy to ask firefighters to respond to such an alarm, just as it's unfair to demand that your body continually respond to threats of danger from events that cannot be tackled now.

Putting it to use.

Use a Richter earthquake or a hurricane scale of 0 to 10 to rate your stress level. Ratings of 1 to 4 indicate that you are relatively safe; ratings of 5 to 7 are dangerous and require the use of your stress energy for fight or flight; ratings of 8 to 10 indicate a major disaster that could be deadly. Most daily stressors are in the lower ranges and can be dismissed in 5 to 30 seconds by exhaling and deciding if it's safe to continue with your daily tasks. The higher stressors of 8 to 10 are rare in most areas of the world and are generally beyond your control. Even so, you can lower stress and worry by promising that you will not turn against yourself even if the worst happens. (See page 123, "Fear of Death: Knowing What You'll Say to Yourself.")

Hot tip.

If you've experienced trauma or extreme danger in the past, as with posttraumatic stress disorder (PTSD), a split-second stress reaction can be triggered by events similar to what caused the original trauma. Lowering the intensity of this form of stress may take repeated experiences of safety. While PTSD is beyond the scope of this book, several therapies have been proven to be effective in reducing symptoms and the frequency of occurrence. Check with your local hospitals, university counseling centers, and county psychological associations for a list of therapists who work with PTSD clients.

Remember, stress is a survival response that prepares you to run for safety, to fight for your life, or go into a freeze state similar to coma in order to conserve energy. In some cases, your mind will ask you if this current situation is similar to what happened in the past, calling for an adrenaline-fueled stress response. It's up to *you*, from your higher brain, to decide the level of danger and how you choose to act. Each time you take command of your *reactions* and *choose how to act*, you strengthen your leadership role and the neural pathways that communicate between the lower, fight-or-flight reptilian brain and your higher, human, prefrontal cortex executive functions. Overriding lower brain reactions strengthens your leadership over your life.

Procrastination*

Between stimulus and response there is a space. In that space is our power to *choose* our response. In our response lies our growth and our freedom.

—Viktor E. Frankl, *Man's Search for Meaning*

Warning Signs of Procrastination

- ❧ You speak in "have tos" and "shoulds." Life feels like a series of obligations.
- ❧ Your perception of time is unrealistic—you're often late or rushed.
- ❧ You're vague about your goals, vision, and values. You lack effective leadership.
- ❧ You feel stressed, frustrated, depressed.

* Based on my book *The Now Habit: Overcoming Procrastination while Enjoying Guilt-Free Play* (New York: Penguin Random House, 2007).

❧ You're afraid of making a mistake; you have low self-worth.

❧ You're waiting to feel confident, decisive, and motivated, and you need to know everything before you take action.

Practical solution.

Shift from the procrastinator's language of inner conflict ("I have to finish all this boring work, but I don't want to") to the producer's ("I am *choosing* to show up and start"). You don't have to want to start a task; as a human being you have a brain with a leadership executive function that enables you to *choose* surgery, complete a difficult training, or to start doing your income tax. You don't have to wait for some part of you to *want* to. You're the leader in your life, making the tough choices. Use your higher brain functions as our ancestors did: to override the lower, animal brain fear of fire.

Imagery.

Imagine four scenes.

SCENE I. Your task is to walk a board that's 30 feet long, 1 foot wide, and 4 inches thick. You have all of the physical, mental, and emotional ability to do the job. You walk the board with no problem.

SCENE 2. The board is now 100 feet above ground, suspended between two buildings. Your task—to walk the board—and your ability remain the same.

What are you feeling and thinking as you contemplate starting the task now? Let's assume that you experience fear of making a mistake that could lead to serious injury or possibly death from falling 100 feet. Your fear is natural, given how you view the task and the consequences of making a mistake.

Yet we've seen you walk the board when it was on the ground. We know you can do it. We're wondering what's stopping you now. Are you procrastinating? Do you have a fear of failure? Are you worried about not doing the task perfectly?

SCENE 3. While stuck 100 feet above ground on a board 1 foot wide, you naturally delay for several minutes as thoughts of self-criticism, shame, and fear run through your awareness. We, the onlookers, don't know your fears, nor do we have your perspective: to us, you look like a procrastinator.

While you think about how you're going to cope, you become aware of the feeling of intense heat behind you. The building supporting your end of the board is now on fire!

What are you thinking about now? Can you take a step toward completing the task? Are you concerned about doing the task perfectly or looking good? Are you now willing to crawl across the board if you have to? Would you shuffle along on your bottom?

You now have a more immediate danger than fear of failure or criticism from others. Somehow you might just go for it and do it at the last minute. This is what you do when you procrastinate on getting started and wait till the night before the deadline to complete the entire task. Now you don't have time to worry about doing it perfectly or about how you look to others. The fire represents the deadline coming so close that you override your usual fears and excuses and start working on the task, regardless of how imperfect you feel.

SCENE 4. The task is the same: you're still 100 feet above the ground, but without the fire. Now you see that there's a strong net 3 feet below the board. How do you feel now that you have a net below the board? Does having a safety net free you from feeling stuck? Can you imagine taking a step forward, knowing that you won't die if you fall or make a mistake? What do you say to yourself as you notice your safety net? You might possibly be saying, "I won't die," "It won't be the end of the world if I make a mistake," or "If I make a mistake and fall, I can try again."

What you say to yourself is your psychological/emotional *safety net*. Choose the phrase you can say to yourself when contemplating an overwhelming or difficult task. Make yourself safe with *you*, regardless of what happens, and you will eliminate procrastination, stress, and anxiety.

Putting it to use.

How you talk to yourself may be hypnotizing your mind and body to feel ambivalent, anxious, rebellious, or depressed. Identify your default phrases—such as "I have to finish all this work; I should have done more; I don't feel motivated; I don't want to"—that tell your mind and body that your life is a long list of obligations that you should rebel against, that you are being controlled by some authority and you should resist, procrastinate, and avoid.

Shift from "I have to finish all this work, do it perfectly, and have no fun" to "I am choosing to start with one step or fifteen minutes" (versus "I have to finish") on a rough draft (versus all the work done perfectly), with plenty of guilt-free play in my schedule (versus "with no fun or with an endless to-do list"). And "my worth is safe with me" (versus my worth will be judged).

Do you give yourself time for guilt-free play, with no have-tos or shoulds? If not, your life becomes a have-to-do list of obligations you feel forced to finish. Giving yourself hours and days of guilt-free play allows you to choose when to start work on a project, break through inertia, and understand something that you didn't know before. You can commit to take on tasks without making them a burden that you will resent and resist, and on which you'll likely procrastinate. Knowing you have fun scheduled later actually can motivate you to start work sooner—to get it out of the way and fully enjoy your playtime, guilt-free. Whenever you're not enjoying your playtime, start work for fifteen minutes on a project you've been avoiding. This will enhance the quality of your playtime and the quality and quantity of your work.

Hot tip.

Procrastination operates like a phobia—a fear, for example, of spiders, elevators, or airplanes. You avoid the feared object or task because it's painful or associated with failure, frustration, or guilt. To overcome a phobia, you slowly approach it by imagining the feared object (or task) and breathing through the first five to thirty seconds, allowing your body to shut off its stress response and shift to your problem-solving, leadership brain. Even those diagnosed with attention deficit disorder (ADD) often find that staying with the task for five to thirty seconds shifts them from feeling stuck to discovering that "something comes to me." When you face fear for more than five seconds without running away, mentally or physically, your brain shifts from avoidance to problem solving, allowing you to build strength against fears and bullies. You'll also be building and strengthening your brain's neural pathways, which lead to productivity and away from old habits of procrastination.

How I Discovered Choice—a Third Place between Have-to and Don't Want to

When I was completing my airborne paratrooper training, I found myself in a C-130 aircraft traveling 150 mph at an altitude of approximately 1500 feet. I was expected to jump out. This was my graduation day from airborne school.

But I couldn't move. I was stuck, just like a procrastinator: held in place by my inner conflict between "You have to jump" and "Forget about it. There's no way I'm jumping out of a perfectly good airplane."

We had trained to step into the doorway of the plane, put our hands on the outside, bend our knees and jump up to break through the 150 mph propeller blast. If you hesitate, the sergeant kicks you out. If you don't fully commit, you could be picked up by the 150 mph wind tunnel, and your body could slam against the outside of the plane, knocking you unconscious and throwing you into a spin that closes your chute.

With all of this in my mind, I watched very carefully as the first man approached the door. I saw him put his hands on the inside of the door, showing, I thought, some ambivalence. Next he looked down instead of up and his body recoiled from the sight of the ground. From this awkward position—hands on the inside, body pulled back from the door, muscles tight—he forced himself to jump. As we were warned, his body was picked up by that 150 mph wind and was slammed against the outside of the plane. Luckily, his chute opened and he landed safely, with only soreness and black-and-blue marks over his entire body to remind him of the consequences of not fully committing to the task.

Thanks to what I learned from the mistakes of my fellow soldier, I made three choices. My first choice was a no-brainer: "I'm not going to do it that way," and I broke free of being stuck in ambivalence and inner conflict. I was equally certain of my second choice: "I'm not going to be kicked out by the sergeant." My third choice was one of fierce determination: "I'm going to maximize my chances of a safe jump." I thrust my hands forward to the outside of the fuselage, got ready to pull forward, and bent my knees to propel myself upward and away from the plane. Everything about me screamed: "This guy is fully committed to jumping from this plane."

Those formerly conflicting parts of me ("You have to" versus "I don't want to") now focused their energies on supporting my goal and empowering my performance.

Choosing to jump worked! I made a perfect jump—the first of five required to graduate from jump school. After a few minutes of floating in the clouds, I landed without a scratch after falling nearly 1500 feet. I looked up at the planes and the other paratroopers and laughed, saying to myself, "There's a third place. It's not just 'you have to' versus 'I don't want to'; there's *choice*!" I had discovered choice.

That discovery of choice at the age of twenty-two has made all the difference in the rest of my life. I had been stuck, unable to move forward because of a battle inside my head between two parts of me. But when I fully *chose* what to do, in spite of fear and self-doubt, those two parts followed my lead and energized my jump. This got me through Vietnam, graduate school, cancer surgery and chemotherapy, writing my doctoral dissertation and my first six books, and countless less dramatic decisions.

At that time, I didn't know about neuropsychology, the levels of the brain, or the executive leadership function of the human prefrontal cortex. But I knew—actually felt throughout my body—the incredible rush of energy that broke me free of inner conflict and supported my leadership vision.

Time Management: Overcoming Lateness and Deadlines

How can I achieve my goals without deadlines?

My client said, "I now realize that focusing on getting something done causes me to freeze up and feel stressed. You were right. But how can I achieve my goals without deadlines? I worry that I'll just keep starting and never know when I'm supposed to finish."

Use your deadlines to create paths back to *startlines*. You will be given deadlines, or you may set them for yourself, but be careful because they can create anxiety—that is, stuck energy. Like goals, deadlines exist in the future, and your body can't get there. This can cause you to feel overwhelmed and stuck with energy that you can't use now. You'll feel stuck and nervous until you bring your mind into the present with your body. Then you can tell your mind and body what to do now—when and where to start, from the present on the path to your deadline.

Deadlines can be problematic unless you "back-time" into the present, where you can start and when you can leave.

Solution. Create start-lines the way a project manager would when managing several projects. Don't worry about finishing; keep starting. The last time you start is when you'll be finished.

EXAMPLE: A flight deadline: the plane leaves at 9 a.m. It's very dangerous to keep only this deadline in your mind because it ignores these necessary start-lines:

- Gates close at 8:45 a.m.
- Boarding starts at 8:15 a.m. at a gate that may be ten or twenty minutes away from the airport entrance.
- Arrive at security between 7:30 and 8 a.m. to get to the gate on time.
- Leave home at 6:30 or 7 a.m., depending on traffic and distance to the airport.
- Awake at 5:30 a.m.
- Start to get to bed by 10 p.m. the night before your flight.
- Start packing bags at 7 p.m. the night before.
- Start booking the flight two to four weeks in advance to avoid last-minute fees.

- Start preparing the presentation weeks in advance of your flight.
- Confirm the needs of your client and payment for expenses.
- Start doing research for presentation one to three months in advance.
- Have passport renewed six months in advance.

Start now. Call the client about your presentation idea four to six months before your flight.

There Are No Enemies, Only Facts

One of my most organized therapy clients (let's call her Alice) surprised me by saying that she needed help overcoming procrastination. She was even finding it difficult to get to work on time. I asked her what had happened.

Alice said, "I have a relatively new job with a new manager, and I'm the only woman in the department. Even though I'm the most productive, I keep getting passed over for promotion. I'm so resentful that I can't get out of bed in the morning and am coming to work at least twenty minutes late. When the manager sees me, we stare and 'shoot daggers' at each other."

This story of "shooting daggers" at each other rang a bell with me, and I told Alice what had happened to me earlier that month.

It was a beautiful spring day, and I had a new book that I was eager to read while enjoying coffee at my favorite café. I walked quickly from my office at the University of California, Berkeley to the café, which was just a few blocks away.

As I continued down the street, eagerly anticipating my coffee break, I noticed a man scowling at me, shooting daggers. He was dressed in combat fatigues, moccasins, and a leather vest. The only dagger I could actually see was a twelve-inch Bowie knife on the left side of his ammo belt and a hatchet on the right side. I felt a rush of stress and adrenaline and was ready to cross the street to get out of his way and away from his hateful gaze. But I didn't want to be intimidated and didn't want to surrender to his version of me, himself, or his combative version of life.

Luckily, I remembered what our sensei (teacher) said in a recent aikido training session: "There are no enemies, no problems, just facts." I repeated a slightly altered version to myself: "I'm not your enemy; I'm not your problem; I'm just a fact, and so are you" and chose to continue walking toward him instead of crossing the street. The man kept glaring at me as he unsnapped the holster of his hatchet. I continued to look him in the eye until we were about twenty feet apart. I continued walking forward. He pulled the hatchet out and held it up in a menacing gesture. I reminded myself of my sensei's words, "I'm not your enemy," and added, "and I'm not your victim." Somehow my refusal to accept his view of our relationship as potential enemies led me to offer him a compliment: "Nice ax: chrome plated and double-headed."

At this point my potential opponent put his ax back into its holster and walked around me. I breathed a sigh of relief and continued on to the café to enjoy a cup of coffee and my new book.

Upon hearing about my experience of shooting daggers, Alice said: "Something like that happened to me a few Sundays ago. I like to take photos around Berkeley on my day off—lots of interesting characters there. I came upon this very intense-looking young man smoking near his motorcycle, dressed in leathers and chains. I asked him if I could take his picture. He got very angry, narrowed his eyes, scowled, reached into his boot, and pulled out a knife, thrusting it toward my face, saying, 'Is this what you wanna see, lady?' I was so intent on getting this great photo that I took his hand holding the knife and said, 'Yes. Could you tilt it this way so it reflects the sun?' And he posed for me like a puppy for ten photos."

To which I said, "Wow, that's amazing. I think you know what you're going to do about your manager tomorrow morning." With the same sense of fearlessness that she displayed when grabbing the young man's knife-holding hand, Alice incorporated her version of "I'm not your enemy; I'm not your problem."

As was his habit, Alice's manager shot daggers at her that next morning; this time she didn't shoot daggers back but simply smiled. She felt more in control and had overcome her procrastination. A few months later, without saying a word about their prior problems, Alice was promoted to manager of her department and became the first woman to hold that position. She wasn't the manager's problem anymore, and he wasn't her problem. As an added bonus, she overcame her resentment and her lateness, and I received one of those ten photos.

Managing Procrastinators

If you've ever tried to herd cats, get teenagers to clean their room, or get a timely response from a procrastinator, you know that your usual management instincts are useless. And yet we all must work with, and live with, individuals whose procrastination problems cause us delays, frustration, missed deadlines, and angry customers. What doesn't work:

Pressure. Putting pressure on procrastinators only backfires. Nagging will only cause resistance and contribute to their procrastination patterns. You need a more strategic approach rather than more of the same.

Commanding. "You have to finish this project. You have to meet this deadline." While this statement seems to make sense, it shows a lack of understanding of the procrastinator's problems with realistic time limits, perfectionism, setting priorities, and feeling overwhelmed.

It adds to the threat of "You have to" (or else) a focus on finishing in the imaginary future without indicating *when to start* or when to deliver periodic drafts and progress reports.

Understanding How Procrastinators Think

Employers, managers, and parents will be more effective in managing procrastinators when they understand how procrastinators think and talk to themselves.

They pressure themselves with "You have to" statements and then resent and resist the authoritarian voices in their heads and in their office.

Procrastinators tell themselves, "I have to finish all this work, do it perfectly, and miss out on all the fun that others have." This form of ineffective self-management makes them more likely to avoid work and give in to the multiple distractions of emails, texts, Google searches, apps, and smartphones.

Procrastinators frighten themselves and cause stress and anxiety, worrying about being judged and possibly fired. They are self-critical and seldom acknowledge when they're doing something right.

Effective Management

Effective managers resist the temptation to contribute to the procrastinator's own form of counterproductive dialogue and behavior.

1. Choice replaces compliance. "You should" and "You have to" messages almost always evoke resistance, resentment, and rebellion that are expressed through procrastination, noncompliance, coming in late, and sometimes even sabotage. To drastically reduce procrastination, offer options to employees that stimulate creative problem solving, cooperation, and motivation.

When they are given clear options rather than demands and threats, employees have been known to willingly contribute cost-saving suggestions and hard work. Smart nurses and doctors have learned to describe the consequences of not following—and the benefits of following—medical directions and then allowing the patient to choose rather than ordering compliance.

2. Focus on starting replaces worry about finishing. Peak performance in sports and on the job requires that your mind be in the present, not on the end of the game. Worrying about finishing overwhelms the mind with the impossible task of jumping into the imaginary future. This causes anxiety as your body tries to get into an imaginary time where all the steps of the project are completed. Your energy is stuck because it can't be used now. We experience this stuck energy as anxiety.

Ask the employee, "When will you *start?*" Effective managers understand the importance of communicating to their employees—and themselves—the specific action steps required to *begin* the task. They understand that overcoming start-up inertia is half the battle. To work optimally, a clear picture is needed of the time, the place, the task, and the freedom to choose to start. That is, you can turn procrastinators into producers by teaching them to focus on, "When can I start?" rather than, "I have to finish."

3. Self-acceptance replaces perfectionism. Criticizing employees will lead some to try to be perfect in a futile attempt to avoid mistakes. Being perfect is, of course, impossible, and the attempt is a terrible waste of time that delays the timely completion of projects. To ensure that an employee doesn't waste time trying to be perfect, say, "Get back to me in three hours with a rough draft so I can give you feedback on what to do next." This method of frequent feedback sessions will also help you clarify your own thoughts about the direction of the project and give you a more accurate estimate of how much time it will take the employee to complete a good-enough draft.

Receiving frequent feedback has been found to help employees monitor their behavior and ensure that they are aligned with your goals and timelines.

4. Use a task focus to replace fear of criticism. To maximum long-term employee efficiency, *catch employees doing something right*, to paraphrase Ken Blanchard's *The One Minute Manager*. Employees who worry, "Is the boss going to be angry at me again?" cannot do their best work. Although an employee's personal insecurity is not the manager's problem, managers can create a safe environment for focusing on improving the product or service rather than worrying about being shamed, demeaned, or fired for making a mistake.

As you communicate to employees or teenagers that you respect their worth and dignity as persons, they will reduce much of the fearful thinking and avoidant behaviors that are the chief causes of procrastination. They will learn to focus more quickly on optimal job performance rather than on the need to be perfect in an attempt to avoid anticipated criticism and shaming.

Loss of Motivation

Practical solution.

Stop waiting for your ego to feel motivated to complete a large project. *Choose to start*, and watch as your natural curiosity leads you to take another step forward to learn more. To paraphrase psychologist Abraham Maslow: human beings have a natural drive to do good work, to make a contribution, and to be fair and just. Maslow says that when this drive is dampened, something in the society has blocked it. Notice the thoughts learned earlier in life that are making you question your ability and to fear mistakes and criticism. Challenge these outdated beliefs and allow your natural motivation to problem-solve and learn carry you forward.

Imagery.

Remember the feeling of walking, jogging, or swimming and how the movement of your arms pulls you forward, how the rolling of your foot from heel to big toe naturally and effortlessly propels you into your next step. Movement generates a natural "motor-vation," moving you forward almost effortlessly. A stone under the wheel of a large truck can cause inertia—a resistance to change or movement—but once the tire moves over the stone, the truck starts to roll and shifts to momentum. Now the once immobile truck, stuck in inertia, is propelled forward. Lack of motivation is similar to that small stone: it's stopping you from moving forward with your life. Getting beyond inertia may feel uncomfortable for a few seconds, but when you stop waiting to feel motivated and take the first step, you'll be rolling along.

Putting it to use.

Notice if you're talking to yourself in have-tos. Or notice when you feel "I don't want to"—indicating that there's a hidden "You have to (or else)" causing resistance. You feel a loss of motivation when you drive with the brakes on, figuratively speaking, by splitting your energies into "You have to" versus "but I don't want to." Loss of motivation happens when your energy is split and stuck in a tug-of-war between these two parts. Feeling stuck causes you to lose your normal drive to solve problems and mysteries or to see a play, a puzzle, or story to its conclusion.

In your natural state, there is no such thing as loss of motivation. All human beings are naturally motivated to learn, to problem-solve, to advance, and to improve their homes and environment.

Breaking Free of Inner Conflict: Choosing to Fight for My First Book

I was incredibly motivated to write my first book: *Coping with the Emotional Impact of Cancer.* I marched the streets of Manhattan, calling publishers and photocopying my book proposal along the way. I was so passionate about the importance of this book that I convinced fifteen publishers to look at my proposal. A few weeks later I received fifteen letters of rejection. They believed that the public wasn't ready for a book about cancer in 1982.

After I recovered from my initial disappointment, I searched for and found an agent who believed in my book as much as I did. She was able to contact the right editor in chief at Bantam, and Bantam bought my book. They paid me an advance, put me on their deadline, and gave me a persnickety editor.

To my astonishment, I lost motivation. I couldn't write for two weeks until I realized that I had begun to tell myself: "You *have to* write for them. It's *their* book. You *have to* meet *their* deadline, and you *have to* put up with this fussy editor."

I had lost ownership of my work, and a part of me was very resentful and resistant, fighting against all the have-to messages I was telling myself. I realized that I needed to fight to regain control over my book. I wanted to break free of the inner conflict between the voices of "You have to" and "I don't want to." I needed to recall what I learned as a new paratrooper when I was stuck and unable to move: there's a third place of choice and determination. So I *chose* to tell the editor that, as the author, I had the right to tell my story my way; I negotiated the deadline and the payment schedule; and I fought to have the word "cancer" in the title. My motivation and excitement about my book returned. I was *choosing* to write *my* book, my way. It was no longer a have-to. I had broken free once again from the inner conflict between have-to versus "I don't want to," and I felt empowered with restored motivation.

It's between You and the Bear

Shortly after my article "Fighting Cancer: One Patient's Perspective" was published in *The New England Journal of Medicine* (Feb. 8, 1979), I was besieged with requests to speak at a variety of medical and healthcare conferences. One memorable event was a presentation to the Arizona Department of Health. The audience was wonderfully receptive and eager to hear how cancer patients can benefit from actively participating in their treatment rather than passively complying. I was very happy that my story of fighting cancer was reaching doctors, nurses, and other healthcare professionals.

To add to my excitement, the local television news crew approached me for an interview at the end of my presentation. The interview went on for longer than usual, so I was led to believe that I would be on the news that evening. When I asked about which time slot, I was told: "It'll be on the six o'clock news. It's between you and the bear that just escaped from the zoo."

Back at my hotel that evening, I eagerly turned on the six o'clock news. To my dismay, the TV anchors were giggling about the cute bear cub running along the freeway. Indeed it was between me and the bear, and the bear won. So much for puffing up my ego for more than a few hours. I keep that memory handy whenever I get a little too full of myself. I remind myself: "Neil, it's between you and the bear."

Goal Achievement

It's not discipline, willpower, or pressure from others that facilitates adherence to a challenging course of action. Rather, it is the freedom to choose among alternatives, the personal commitment to a mission, and the willingness to take responsibility for the consequences of one's decisions, that steels the will and emboldens the spirit.

—NEIL FIORE, *Coping with the Emotional Impact of Cancer*

Practical solution.

Create a three- and four-dimensional path—over distance and time—back from your goal and deadline to the start-line today. Commit to start work on each step along the path, on every course in your school's curriculum, on each chapter of your book, on each customer.

Practice shifting from feeling overwhelmed to being focused in one strong exhalation—like a karate shout. Choose your path to the goal; when you reach your initial goal, you'll find more paths, more goals. Once again, back-time to your start line and take your first step.

Imagery.

See the path to your goal as a trail up a mountain. Plan where you will rest and when you'll recalculate your climb. Evaluate what you're learning as you gain new information and a new perspective, and get smarter. Notice how you adapt to the altitude and make changes to your goals as you gain new information along your journey. Your future self will know more than you know now at the start of your journey. You can't know everything at the start.

Putting it to use.

Commit to the path to your ultimate goal—what you want to achieve. To be efficient and successful, you'll need to create a *functional* goal that tells your mind and body what to do as you start to work on the tasks along the path to your goal. For example: to graduate from school (your ultimate goal), you must take courses and pass exams along the path. It is insufficient (and counterproductive) to simply want the ultimate goal.

Your mind and body need to know your *functional* goal—your commitment to show up for each exam and to focus on each question. If your ultimate goal is to complete a marathon, your functional goal would be to commit to taking every step and stride along the path, every mile, in spite of self-doubts and fatigue.

Hot tip.

Before committing to a goal and its path, consider the pros and cons: the risks and benefits of pursuing the goal and all the steps along the way. This will strengthen your courage and mental toughness when things get difficult.

To ensure that your goal is more than just another New Year's resolution that will fade within a month, prepare and rehearse a plan for getting back on track if you deviate from your commitment.

- Know what you will do when there are setbacks or distractions.
- Rehearse recommitting to your goal and path if you experience a setback.
- Anticipate how you might feel and what you usually say to yourself.
- Be prepared to stop self-criticism and self-doubt.
- Resist the urge to throw away all the progress you've made over the last thirty to sixty days just because of one slip or lapse.

❧ Keep building on your progress and add another day of commitment tomorrow.

Preparing to Run a Marathon

My first book was due to be published in September 1984. I thought it would be a brilliant idea to run the San Francisco Marathon at the same time. I started training in February and progressed from my usual fifteen miles per week all the way up to forty-five miles.

I learned that running a healthy marathon requires training runs of at least sixty miles per week. If I was to avoid hitting the "wall"—that infamous sudden loss of energy at mile eighteen or twenty caused by the depletion of glycogen from the liver and muscles—and possibly ruining my health, I would need to get beyond my plateau of forty-five miles per week. But where was I going to find more time to run, put in forty to fifty hours on my job, plus devote twenty hours to finishing the last drafts of my book?

Resistance to both writing and running set in bigtime. I began to have nightmares that I would run twenty-six miles of a marathon, and, instead of the expected ribbon signaling the finish of the course, I saw officials telling me I had to run another 385 yards. Those additional 385 yards were in fact added prior to the 1908 Olympic Marathon in London so it could finish under the royal box of the king and queen of England at the stadium. My body refused to run another step, just as my mind was resisting my editor's re-writes of my manuscript. (By the way, I may have imagined it, but I did feel that my editor resembled Queen Victoria.)

My dreams were telling me to reclaim control over my book and decide if and how I would train for the marathon. I needed to break through my resistance to the 385 yards added to the marathon for the king and queen of England and to my editor's repeated changes of my book.

A new strategy came to me: at the end of my Saturday nine-mile run, I could add an additional 385 strides, counting each step uphill, *choosing* to take those extra steps. This exercise actually helped me make breakthroughs in my writing as I wondered what solutions would come to me for my book before I reached the top of that seemingly impossible hill.

My body was also trying to tell me something about the foolishness of running a marathon (at least for me). During my six months of training, I experienced several injuries—shin splints, swollen knees, sore feet—that led me to reexamine the wisdom of putting my body through the 26.2-mile run. I decided I would change my goal to one of learning how to listen to and work with my body within the limited time I had.

I decided that a healthier goal for me would be to run a half-marathon: 13.1 miles. It would be less damaging and more appropriate for my limited training schedule of forty-five miles per week. Perhaps I was lucky, but I ran half of the marathon in 1984 and finished feeling great, while friends who forced themselves through the wall got sick; some of them never ran again. The half-marathon was a perfect distance for me and my knees. Happily, I was able to run three more before switching over to biking.

Imagine if this principle was applied to climbing Mount Everest or other life-threatening goals. Sure, your goal is to get to the top, but when you see that the weather conditions have changed and people could die, wouldn't you change your goal to making sure everyone on the expedition survives and returns home safely? Unfortunately, there are multiple examples of unnecessary deaths on Mount Everest (over three hundred since 1922) because of the egos of a few who were unable to change their goals to meet the reality of changing conditions.

Worry

Practical solution.

Promise yourself that you will not make yourself miserable if you don't get what you want, don't achieve your goal, or lose something or someone. The underlying cause of worrying is the fear that you will hate yourself. Promise not to hate yourself if things don't go your way. Plan on becoming the kind of person who says, "I don't worry because regardless of what happens, I know I will be at peace with myself. I will not make myself more miserable."

Imagery.

Create a plan for how you will cope if what you're worried about happens. Include a plan for recovery from regret, sadness, or depression.

Plan what you will do if something disrupts your plans.

Plan who you will call to support you. Rehearse what you will say.

Plan how you will carry on even if you don't feel like it or don't want to.

Plan to overcome the "what-if" thoughts and feelings that are your default reactions.

Putting it to use.

Your worrying mind wants to know your plan for dealing with an anticipated (or imagined) problem.

Use plans to calm your worrying mind. A plan communicates to the lower brains: "The leader (the executive function of the human brain) has shown up. I got this. You are not alone and are not responsible for my life. I'm taking responsibility for this plan."

Planning also creates neural pathways that prepare your brain to take corrective action if something negative happens. Plans are a form of mental rehearsal to keep you on track if something unexpected takes place. They prepare you to perform optimally and to override your usual default or fear reactions.

Plans also communicate to your worrying mind that you are paying attention to its concerns and are stepping up to take action, allowing this survival function to turn down the volume on its fear and screaming.

Schedule a time to do "quality worrying" to answer the what-if questions. Instead of worrying every hour, all day long, schedule a time to do some *quality worrying*. Set aside a few minutes at a specific time to answer all the what-if questions with a plan that says, "This is what I will do if that happens." Instead of trying to ignore potential problems, do a mental rehearsal of how to face and deal with your worst fears and most persistent worries.

Setting a time for quality worrying shuts off worrying during the day and allows you to focus on tasks and develop effective plans. You may be amazed, as I was, that your worrying mind will actually follow your schedule.

Create the ultimate plan to stop worry and shift to wonder. The ultimate or overarching plan makes this guarantee: "Regardless of what happens, your worth is safe with me. I will not make you feel bad. I will not turn against you just because something goes wrong."

Your ultimate plan for survival maintains a solid sense of worth regardless of what happens. It answers the what-if questions with "Even if the worst happens, even if they turn against you, I'm on your side; I will not make you feel bad."

What is your plan for making yourself safe with *you*? How many worries would disappear if you could guarantee that—regardless of what happens—you will forgive and accept yourself? Remember that accepting yourself as a human being who cannot control everything is the ultimate plan that integrates and quiets your worrying mind.

The ultimate plan is that, regardless of what happens, you guarantee your worth will be safe with you.

Hot tip.

Whenever you're relaxed and at peace, press a finger to your thumb to record this memory. Then inhale, hold your breath, exhale, and float down into the support of the chair, the floor, or the bed as you relax your fingers. Press this memory into your fingers, nerves, and muscles—making it a button to be accessed whenever you start to worry. Carry with you this moment of inner peace, free from worry. Go from worry to wonder as you wonder how your subconscious inner genius will work on this issue for you and bring you a solution in your daydreams or nighttime dreams.

Frustration

Frustration can be defined as:

- 🍃 Struggling to control something beyond your control
- 🍃 The feeling of anger or annoyance caused by being unable to do something you desperately want to do
- 🍃 The inability to master a new skill, such as operating a new computer program or your new phone
- 🍃 Being prevented from reaching your goals or fulfilling your needs
- 🍃 The annoyance that comes when placed on "hold" for over twenty minutes while being told they're taking care of other customers

Practical solution.

When you feel stuck and blocked from reaching your goal or destination, let go of trying to control something that is beyond your control. Let go of trying to be godlike, with infinite power and responsibility. Accept that you are a human being with limited control and limited power. This also works for reducing inappropriate or undeserved guilt feelings.

Stop trying so hard. Stop pushing on the "pull" door. Let go and discover that the door pulls open easily. If it won't open or turn easily, you're probably turning or pushing in the wrong direction. It was meant to turn and open easily. Life has hinged the door so it opens easily. Stop pushing against life.

Acknowledge that you are not in control of other people, traffic, the weather, or the government. Shift your focus to what you can do now. Ask yourself: "What can I do *now?*"

Move from struggle and worry to an action that is under your control. Let go of what you can't do, but do something!

Imagery.

Imagine you're driving on the highway. You feel frustrated by the other drivers because they seem too slow or too reckless, and you can't make them follow your advice. They won't listen to you, and they don't drive the way you want them to drive. They don't seem to understand or even want your generous advice. You tighten your fists, grit your teeth, curse, raise your blood pressure, and set yourself up for a possible heart attack. Or you can just let go of trying to control other people and focus your very real power on choosing your attitude.

Putting it to use.

When I hear my clients say, "I'm frustrated," I ask what may sound like a strange question: "How are you frustrating yourself?"

If you're feeling frustrated, you could benefit from asking yourself the same question, which implies that you play some part in starting or maintaining this aggravating feeling.

But how? When you try to control something beyond your control or attempt to be in some imaginary time—such as the future, when the effects of the current problems might be significantly reduced—you will feel frustrated. You can't get into the imaginary future to solve the problem; you can't magically appear at your desired destination or goal. You're stuck waiting in the present. Your refusal to accept this fact leads to feelings of exasperation and anger. Feelings of frustration lessen when you accept that you are not a god, a superwoman, or superman. Let go of this illusion of superpowers and accept yourself as a human being.

Frustration means you are in a tug-of-war with reality; let go of your end of the rope, and the tension will subside.

Hot tip.

Every time you feel frustrated, tighten your fists and hold your breath. Then release your fists into an open-handed position and exhale as you let go of trying to control something beyond your control. In an open-handed gesture, accept that you are human and therefore not in control of everything. Take control of the one thing always under your control: your attitude and how you make yourself feel.

Depression

A human being is a part of the whole that we call the universe. . . . [Yet] he experiences himself . . . as something separated from the rest—a kind of optical illusion of his consciousness . . . a prison. . . . Our task must be to free ourselves from this prison by widening our circle of compassion to embrace all living beings and all of nature.   —ALBERT EINSTEIN

Practical solution.

Have compassion for the part of you that feels depressed. Replace "I am depressed" with "A part of me feels depressed" or, "I'm noticing feelings of depression." It's dangerous (and inaccurate) to define yourself by your occupation, a disease, a diagnosis, or a single feeling.

You are more than the feeling of depression. *You are the one who notices it with compassion and understanding.*

Shift to being the one that *notices* feelings—from your higher Self, your executive function, your higher brain. From that perspective, choose what to do and how you will make yourself feel this evening, even though a part of you is feeling sadness or depression.

Imagery.

Five people are hit by rocks.

1. One says, "Everyone hates me."
2. Another says, "I'm always the one who gets hit with rocks."
3. Another says, "Why am I getting hit with rocks? What's wrong with me?"
4. Another says, "I don't like getting hit with rocks. I'm getting out of here."
5. The fifth one says, "Life has falling rocks, asteroids, and ice cream. I accept life even when it hurts."

It's not the events (or rocks) of life that determine how we feel, but how we interpret them.

There is nothing either good or bad but thinking makes it so.

—WILLIAM SHAKESPEARE, *HAMLET*, ACT 2, SCENE 2

Putting it to use.

When things go wrong—that is, when they don't go your way—you may feel an initial twinge of hurt and regret; that's normal and almost unavoidable. What you do next is under your control. Don't deny the hurt, sad, or depressed feeling; integrate it into your larger self and your higher vision. Acknowledge feelings with a "Yes, and . . .": "Yes, that *was* awful, and *now* I'm choosing to recommit to my vision, my goals, my values, and to reaffirm my life."

Notice what's around you and what you feel physically. Notice what you see, smell, and hear: the sky is blue or grey; the trees are in bloom; my legs feel strong; the birds are singing; the air smells sweet after the rain. You can expand your awareness to include more than just a sad feeling or pain. As you notice more around you, your sadness is held in a larger space and thus becomes smaller in comparison. It is no longer all that you feel.

Hot tip.

Plan a funeral and burial for a sad past event, relationship, or idealized family member. Consider how and when you will bury, burn, or throw into the sea an item, photo, or letter that represents that past event or person. Record the date of the burial as you would on a tombstone or crypt. Whenever feelings or thoughts about that event or person recur, imagine and remember the date you buried it. Your brain will soon catch up to your feelings and let it go.

An advanced practice. Mourn the loss of your old default identity: bury it, release it, exhale it away; expect a new, integrated, higher Self. Accept the limits of your human control. Mourning is an act of humility that shows compassion for the human condition and courage to go on with our lives, even though we now know we are vulnerable to loss and that our future holds both more loss and more joy.

Coping with Loss: The Loss of a Chapter

The loss of a morning's work on the chapter of a book doesn't compare to the loss of a loved one, a home, a job, or a much-loved pet, but it will illustrate some key points of coping with loss.

My morning started off with an unusual burst of creativity. In less than three hours, I had completed almost an entire chapter of what was to become my book *The Now Habit*. Then the electricity went out, my computer went down, and I lost all that "brilliant" work.

A spate of thoughts came to me: "Didn't you back it up?" "Maybe it's still on the hard drive." "How could that happen?" I've heard it all before and, as I psychologist, I realize this is a way of coping with, or possibly denying, your own vulnerability to a similar calamity. No, it wasn't backed up. It was truly lost.

I shouted to the heavens, "I can't believe this. How could this happen to me?" The heavens seemed to answer back: "Believe it. It can happen to you." Then I went through the first four of Elisabeth Kübler-Ross's stages of loss: denial, anger, bargaining, and depression. I took my computer to a repair shop and learned that my chapter could not be retrieved. I also learned that a twelve-year-old boy had released a Mylar kite into a power station and shut down half of the city. Again I raged at the heavens: "I don't believe this. I lost my work to a twelve-year-old with a kite!" I think I saw the clouds part as the heavens once again reminded me, "Believe it." I replied, "And you expect me to continue to write for that idiot publisher knowing this can happen again?" The imagined (or hallucinated) voice repeated, "Believe it."

Humbled by this loss, I slowly moved to Kübler-Ross's fifth stage: acceptance. I was required to accept the loss not only of the chapter but of my illusion of invulnerability. This could happen to me and no doubt would happen again in spite of all the safeguards I was now putting in place. Acceptance means acknowledging that you are human and are therefore vulnerable to loss, pain, joy, and creativity. Accepting yourself as human—and therefore vulnerable to loss—is one of the fastest ways I know of to cope with loss and ride through the sadness.

Depression has been called a refusal to mourn—a holding on to the past. This refusal to let go keeps us stuck in depression, whereas mourning our loss—letting go of what happened in the past—allows us to proceed to a more manageable sadness that is a normal part of our human experience.

Coping with the Physical Pain of Depression

I know the voice of depression
Still calls to you.
I know those habits that can ruin your life
Still send their invitations. . . .

O keep squeezing drops of the Sun
From your prayers and work and music
And from your companion's beautiful laughter

And from the most insignificant movements
Of your own holy body.

Now, sweet one,
Be wise.
Cast all your votes for Dancing!
—Hafiz (1320–89), "Cast All Your Votes for Dancing"

Shortly after my father and grandfather died, a friend lost his leg to cancer, my girlfriend broke up with me, and one of my grad school professors was giving me a hard time. I felt miserable. Not only did I feel emotionally depressed, I felt a severe pain in my stomach that bent me over as I made myself tread across the campus of the University of Maryland. I was oblivious to the beauty of the trees and grass of the campus. My awareness was completely dominated by depression and pain.

My next class was uphill, and as I tried to climb forward, my feet felt as if they were bound by lead weights. I was entirely absorbed by the sadness of my life until I heard a loud noise, like a firecracker, and looked up. I saw before me the trees, grass, dogs running after frisbees, a blue sky, and animated students rushing to their next class. I still felt the depression and pain, but now it was contained in a larger world that was fully alive and beautiful. Now the depression became a bit smaller. I said to myself, "Yes, you feel depressed, *and* the campus is green and alive, your legs are strong and walking, you're breathing fresh air, and the pain in your stomach has shrunk to the size of a grapefruit."

As I advanced uphill to my next class, I continued to include more in my awareness: thoughts about other classes I'd be taking with friendlier professors, other friends I had, when I'd return home at semester break. Each additional thought took its place in my awareness, leaving less room for the previously all-consuming depression. By the time I got to my next class, the pain of depression was still there, but now, instead of controlling my total awareness, it was the size of an orange that I could comfortably carry with me.

When you're in pain, it cries out for attention, calling for action to fix or heal the injury. Pain can be all-consuming, as if there's nothing else in your world but torment. While you need to acknowledge pain and take action to address it, you can limit its power over your full awareness. You can put physical and emotional pain in a larger context that helps lessen its intensity and its command of your awareness. You can see, feel, and smell what's around you just as that firecracker woke me up to the vibrant life and beauty of the campus.

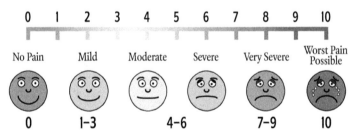

You can also assign a number to your depression on a scale of 0 to 10, as in the accompanying pain diagram, where 0 represents no pain and 10 is the worst pain possible. This will allow you to see how the pain changes over time and to notice which thoughts and activities make it better or worse.

Inner Peace

Practical solution.

Commit to inner peace and freedom from self-induced stress. Consider making inner peace a strong magnetic path that pulls you back on track whenever you deviate from your mission. Say "Stop" to stressful thoughts.

Imagery.

Imagine you have a protective atmosphere all around you—three feet in front, behind, to the left and right, above and below you. It is thick enough to burn up negative thoughts, insults, and words before they reach your heart, just the way the earth's atmosphere burns up most meteorites before they reach the earth's surface.

Make your home a sanctuary, free of the dust and the stresses of the outside world. Your body and mind are also your home and can be made free of stress and worry within five to thirty seconds as you imagine being within a protective sanctuary.

Putting it to use.

To reinforce your leadership in protecting your unique version of life, you can use a version of a three-finger exercise adapted from *Trance and Treatment* by Herbert and David Spiegel.

Prepare three statements along the lines of:

1. Raise your thumb and say, "This is my life." (You might add, "This is my body. This is my career.") Take ownership of your life, body, and career. Alternatively: "I'm grateful for my own unique version of life expressing itself through me. I'm grateful for my body and all that it endures and does for me."

2. Raise your first finger, press it to your thumb, and say, "Certain habits, substances, or relationships are toxic to the full expression of my life and the full vitality of my body."

3. Press your middle finger and first finger to your thumb and say to yourself: "I am committed to protecting my life and body from all toxic fears, habits, relationships, and substances." Or, "I am committed to experiencing the full expression of my life and my body." That is, adopt a protective leadership role for your life and your body.

Take a deep breath and hold it as you commit to protecting your body and your life from toxic substances, habits, and relationships. Exhale and release your fingers. You can use the pressing of your thumb to your first two fingers as a reminder throughout the day of your active leadership role as protector of your life and your body whenever you want to break an unhealthy habit or thought.

The Power of Inner Peace

My book *Awaken Your Strongest Self* is my most psychologically challenging and ambitious work. It required a prestigious agent who could sell the concepts to publishers. I found such an agent in New York with offices located at Rockefeller Center overlooking the skating rink, the statue of Atlas, and St. Patrick's Cathedral. Even before I got to her office, I knew this could be my biggest book deal yet. I overheard the receptionist talking to a TV personality about seeing his show; I noticed that every office was elegantly appointed, and each had its own fireplace. This was a high-class, top-drawer, big-league operation.

My new agent invited me into her office, had coffee brought in, and proceeded to point out the books of her other authors: that one earned an advance of

$250,000; this one $500,000; that one $350,000. Needless to say, I was impressed and excited. We planned to go over the details the next morning at an uptown restaurant.

I had flown into Newark Airport from California to stay at my mom's home in Jersey City, not anticipating the need to be in Manhattan the next morning. I got up early, dressed in my best suit, white shirt, and tie and was eager to take my rental car on the road. One big problem: the left rear tire was flat. Typically, I would have gotten angry at myself for not booking a hotel in Manhattan and possibly screwing up what could be my biggest book deal.

But that year I had made a commitment to inner peace: regardless of what happens, I would be calm and focused. This flat tire provided an excellent test of my resolve. I was pulled off track for five to ten seconds (that's one to two breaths), but my commitment to inner peace brought me back. I didn't have time for self-blame and self-doubt; I was on a mission. I took a few deep breaths, opened the car's trunk, and proceeded to look for the jack and spare tire. There was a jack, but instead of a regular tire, there was one of those small doughnut-shaped temporary replacement tires. Surprise, surprise: it also was flat!

This time I was ready to lose it, and would have if it weren't for my commitment to inner peace. The usual curses and negative thoughts of failure ran through my head, but I was committed to make this work. Pulling my mind in toward the magnetic path of inner peace helped me think clearly about problem solving: I called the restaurant in New York and told them to pass on the message that I might be thirty minutes late. I folded my jacket in the back seat of the car, rolled up the sleeves of my shirt, and walked that flat spare tire to the nearest gas station, where I inflated it. Now all I had to do was jack up the rental car, remove the old tire, and put on the newly inflated spare tire.

This, however, was only half the battle. The next challenge was driving on the New Jersey Turnpike through the Lincoln Tunnel using a small, reserve doughnut-shaped tire. I drove as fast as I dared on that spare tire and stayed in the far-right lane, but the other drivers were tailgating and beeping their horns all the way. I repeatedly tapped into my mission, taking deep breaths every few minutes.

Somehow I was able to reach the approach to the Lincoln Tunnel and could see that the long line of backed-up of cars would make me late by at least an hour. I needed to take a few more deep breaths and recommit to inner peace as I attempted to move to the right through lines of angry drivers so I could get out of the lane to the tunnel and attempt to find a ferry from Weehawken or Hoboken.

Now I was doubling back south a few miles in hopes of finding the sign for the ferry that I had seen from the turnpike. There it was: "Weehawken Ferry Terminal," with plenty of parking. Once I got on the ferry, I timed the ride at eight minutes to reach Manhattan and another ten-minute taxi ride to the restaurant. And all of it like an exhilarating episode of *Mission Impossible*— only protected within a sanctuary of inner peace.

Mission accomplished! I arrived for my meeting with my new agent and was reassured when I saw her smile and heard her say, "You're only ten minutes late."

Lack of Confidence

Practical solution.

Stop waiting for your ego to feel confident. Choose to show up and start working. Your ego identity may never get past the confidence level of your sixteen-year-old self. It's up to *you*, today, to choose to take risks, knowing you have a guarantee that your worth as a person is secure with you.

Even when a part of you is holding on to the memory of failure and feelings of low self-esteem, start making leadership decisions, using your "new" human brain and strongest Self to move forward. You'll prove to yourself that a lack of confidence doesn't have to stop you from facing your fears and starting over again.

Talk to the part of you that lacks confidence: "You don't have to know how to do it all. All you really need to do is to show up, focus on starting, and watch yourself go from not knowing to knowing. Fear and lack of confidence can't stop our commitment to this mission. I've got this!"

Imagery.

Remember when you heard yourself say, "I don't know what to do. I don't know what to say. I lack confidence." Yes, a part of you may feel like an impostor and doesn't know what to do. Once you get started doing something—even if it's imperfect—you'll know more than you know now. Watch as you shift from not knowing to knowing, from lack of confidence to the courage that comes when you take your first steps.

Regardless of what happened in the past to weaken your confidence, the only place you can work toward a solution is in the present.

Shift from thinking about past failures (or anticipated failures in the future) to what you can do now. Start doing something now for fifteen to thirty minutes that will increase your chances of success. Once you break through the fear and inertia, decide if you're ready to invest five to ten hours this week (one to two hours a day) to start making progress in improving your work habits, exam taking skills, or your commitment to exercise and healthy eating.

The point is: focusing on what you can do *now* will gain you more than waiting to feel confident. You'll feel more confident *after* you get started; you'll know more than you know now, and you'll even feel motivated to continue learning and making greater progress.

Putting it to use.

Notice when your self-doubting voice shows up. Does it say: "I don't know what to do. I can't do it. I lack confidence," or "Easier said than done"?

What will you say to that voice?

Replace "Easier said than done" with "OK, sounds difficult, but I'm choosing to start and to see how it goes" or "This will be interesting, because I haven't the foggiest idea of how I'll get it done."

Yes, the actual starting, doing, and getting it done will take effort. But does it have to be easy for you to even contemplate giving it your best shot? Are you afraid of failure, difficulty, or self-criticism? You're not going to let that bully *fear* stop you, are you?

Practice going from not-knowing to knowing by doing sudoku or a jigsaw or crossword puzzle. On the first day, it's impossible to solve; then you see one line of a solution. Two or three days later, you've completed the entire puzzle—going from impossible to possible, from not-knowing to knowing. That's the power of facing the unknown and getting started rather than waiting to feel confident.

Jack Passes the State Bar Exam

Jack failed the state bar exam three times. He was humiliated and was about to give up. He explained his inability to get back on his feet again by saying, "I lack confidence." He was understandably discouraged and a *part* of him did not feel confident that he could make himself study again, go through three days of testing, and pass on a fourth attempt.

I told Jack I had to ask him a dumb question: "Are you going to take the bar exam again?" He said, "Yes, that is a dumb question. And yes, I *am* going to take it again."

I said, "If you're going to take the exam again, stop confusing your mind and body with 'have to,' as if you're a victim who's doing it against his will."

With a few sessions of help, Jack shifted from the inner conflict of "I have to take the bar exam again" to "I'm *choosing* to show up on every question for each of the three days of the exam." He *chose* to show up, *chose* to confront each question, *demanding* another opportunity to demonstrate what he knew about the law and his ability to be a knowledgeable lawyer.

Now Jack was fully *committed* to performing optimally on each question for each of the eighteen hours. He stayed focused on doing what he could do, ready to turn aside the nagging voice in the back of his mind that continually asked, "But what if you fail?" He was prepared with the answer, "Regardless of what happens, I won't let it be the end of the world for us. I won't make you feel bad. You can feel confident that your worth is safe with me."

Not only did Jack pass the bar exam, but this time he actually enjoyed answering the three days of questions. This time he was showing up as the leader in his life with a clear, chosen commitment to demonstrate what he could do.

Hot tip.

In the words of Theodore Roosevelt:

Dare greatly: It is not the critic who counts; not the man who points out how the strong man stumbles, or where the doer of deeds could have done them better. The credit belongs to the man who is actually in the arena, whose face is marred by dust and sweat and blood; who strives valiantly; who errs, who comes up short again and again, because there is no effort without error and shortcoming; but who does actually strive to do the deeds; who knows great enthusiasms, the great devotions; who spends himself in a worthy cause; who at the best knows in the end the triumph of high achievement, and who at the worst, if he fails, at least fails while daring greatly, so that his place shall never be with those cold and timid souls who neither know victory nor defeat.

Academy Award winner Olympia Dukakis has said that she actively seeks out those activities that cause her to feel a lack of confidence: "I look for things that really scare me to death. If I haven't a clue how to tackle it, if it feels overwhelming, if it feels impossible to do, that's the thing I'm interested in."

Stop waiting to feel confident—act now!

Dare Greatly!

Low Self-Esteem

Practical solution.

Whenever you feel lowered by others or events in your life, make a conscious choice to hold your head up high and refuse to take on the identity of someone who has been lowered. Low self-esteem manifests itself in feelings of worthlessness, feeling inadequate in social situations or incapable of accomplishing any demanding tasks, anticipating failure, pessimism, and sometimes depression. Fredric Neuman, MD, director of the Anxiety and Phobia Center at White Plains Hospital in New York, has written that those suffering from low self-esteem do not respond well to antidepressants because they are not suffering from an illness but from long-held beliefs leading to misconceptions about themselves. Treatment, Dr. Neuman states, needs to be focused on changing these negative ideas.

You may have seen a dog that has been punished or chastised put its head down and its tail between its legs as a signal that it will not fight. Lowering oneself is a survival mechanism for animals: it lowers testosterone and aggression and shows larger animals that you are not a threat. In humans, the signal is the raising of both hands to show that you surrender, that you are not a problem, and that you are not going to fight.

If you've been demeaned as a child by parents, teachers, or bullies, you might have taken on surrender and lowering as part of your personality and come to believe and feel that you are lower than others. To overcome this early conditioning, you might start today to choose to hold your head up high and to override your animal brain's programming. Start the practice of listing your positive qualities to replace thoughts about the negative qualities you've been taught.

Imagery.

Animals have a survival response called *yielding* that keeps them out of fights they can't win. You may have felt this survival instinct when you were surprised by a barking or growling dog. It's natural, and part of your animal brain survival mechanism, to lower your head when you fear being attacked. Once you know you're safe, you have a chance to shake off the alarm and raise your head, walking forward like a human being with your head held high.

Putting it to use.

Notice when you feel lowered by others, by bullies, or by authority figures. Accept a few seconds of lowering as part of your animal brain survival instincts, without taking on low self-esteem as part of who you are. Acknowledge this instinctual response; notice it from your higher, human Self and decide when it's safe to raise your head—and possibly your voice—to defend yourself or to continue on to safety.

Hot tip.

Refuse to be intimidated by critics. Critics and competitors may be envious that you have achieved more than they have. Some may be jealous of you for being in the spotlight or for being more willing than they are to put in the work necessary to succeed. You may remind them of how they failed to live up to their potential. Others just want to share the spotlight and feel they need to bring you down to their level. These weak predator types tend to show up when you succeed at something. Don't give them the power to ruin your evening.

Remember Eleanor Roosevelt's statements: "No one can make you feel inferior without your consent" and "Do what you feel in your heart to be right—for you'll be criticized anyway."

Mourning the Loss of an Idealized Childhood

I suspect that the ungrieved grief keeps you living a half-life. I don't think your soul is able to relax because you're holding on so tight ... and the loss of dreams, the losses of childhood, the losses of the heart go ungrieved because (you think) you have to just keep pressing forward.   —ANNE LAMOTT

Consider the inner conflict experienced by Greg (note: all client names and characteristics have been changed to protect their confidentiality), a successful fifty-two-year-old real estate salesman, who was procrastinating on facing five years of back taxes and innumerable documents from his ex-wife's lawyer. Though Greg always had been organized and conscientious in handling the details of his business, he found it nearly impossible to do any paperwork after his mother died and his wife divorced him.

Greg's mother had become ill a year after his birth and was unable to take care of him. His father, a workaholic with a drinking problem, was seldom around and fought constantly with his wife until they divorced when Greg was six. For most of his childhood, Greg felt pressured to please others in order to avoid abuse, criticism, and rejection. He grew to be a worrier and a pleaser, careful about not showing too much of his true feelings for fear of making someone angry at him.

When he started dating, he was drawn to women who, like his mother, were emotionally unavailable and often angry with him. Ultimately he married a very distant and domineering woman. This kept a regressed, needy part of him striving to win the loving gaze of his aloof mother and to prove that he was worthy of being loved.

When the two women who had controlled and dominated most of his life were gone, Greg unleashed years of the suppressed anger and rebellion of the two-year-old part of himself—the rebellious voice of "I don't want to." He took out some of that anger against a major symbol of a controlling authority figure for many people: the Internal Revenue Service.

Ironically, having been freed of external authorities, Greg now was being controlled by an inner battle between his own internal voice of authority—a six-year-old "superego," authoritarian voice who coped by learning his mother's have-tos—and the "I don't want to's" of his newly liberated two-year-old. Now, in spite of what his adult self knew was irrational, Greg was acting like a child who refused to do anything that seemed like homework imposed by parents, teachers, lawyers, or the government. He had regressed to his two-year-old rebel.

In our executive coaching sessions, Greg wanted me to make him stop procrastinating and make sure he did his back taxes and legal forms. But I refused to play this authoritarian role of the six-year-old ("you have to" voice) because I knew that it would only keep us stuck in a tug-of-war in which he would play the role of the rebellious two-year-old. In our first meeting, I conscientiously avoided the "have-to" and the "no, you can't" statements of an authority figure. Instead, I modeled for Greg the voice of an executive Self who was secure enough to hear and empathize with all of his anger and resentments: "Of course a part of you doesn't want to do any more work for some parent or boss who's been abusive to you. That's perfectly understandable."

I wanted Greg to know that while he was stuck in the perspective of either child, this terrible task would seem impossible. So, using reverse psychology, I asked him to seriously consider giving up and accepting whatever financial and jail penalties might be imposed. I suggested that filing so many forms and dealing with material from his ex-wife's lawyer and for this departed mother's estate was filled with too much emotion and resentment for him to ever complete it alone. "Completing five years of back taxes, even without the extra emotional burden, is virtually impossible for the average person," I said.

This tactic showed Greg how he might take the "third chair" of his underdeveloped executive Self and empathize with his own rebellious feelings, listen to his worrying mind, and give himself some choices. Although all the choices were unpleasant, they were real choices: continue to pay fines, lose everything and go to jail, or complete the income tax forms. I said, "From the overwhelmed child's perspective, doing all that work seems impossible. But acting from your executive role, you might see some advantages in *choosing* to face such an insurmountable challenge. If the executive *you* really *chooses* to undertake this challenge, you might unite all parts of yourself and tap into resources you don't even know you have. You'll come out on the other side of this journey with all parts of you integrated around a mature Self, and you'll finally be in charge of your life. You'll have learned how to reclaim parts of you frozen away years ago in childhood and make available to you the child's creative spirit to rekindle your own sense of a true Self."

Empathizing with the Child You Were

> I discovered that many people who could not relate to their feelings of hurt, fear, helplessness, anger, or sorrow in a helpful, compassionate way *could* do so when they saw these feelings as belonging to the child still alive within them.
>
> —JOHN WELWOOD, *Reflection and Presence*

Once Greg identified how the experiences of his childhood kept him stuck repeating old patterns, he felt an adult's sense of protection toward the child he was. Now he was able to empathize with a child who had to be so careful not to make his parents upset and to suppress so much of his true self.

I asked Greg, "What do you want that child to know? How will you protect him now and speak up for him in such a way that he can relax his old ways of protecting himself? If you were his coach, father, or guardian angel, how would you lead him out of the self-destructive resentment he's stuck in now?"

Greg thought for a moment, and then, with tears in his eyes, said: "I would tell him: It's over. It's not your fault. I will never let you be controlled like that by anyone ever again. I'm strong enough now to do the right work to get us out of this mess. You can relax. I got this!

I now have better ways to fight back than by cutting off your nose to spite your face."

By the time we completed our first few coaching sessions, Greg's executive Self had been awakened to make the difficult decisions and create a plan, allowing the voice of the rebellious two-year-old to quiet down. After a few more meetings, Greg learned to take the perspective of a leader who could accept the two-year-old's wants and fears without judging them wrong or crazy and without being controlled by them. To truly heal, Greg also needed to help that child in him to mourn the loss of a mother who was only able to give him what he needed during his first years of life. This idealized mother—and his idealized childhood—had died to him long before his actual mother died. If he was to stop repeating the pattern of trying to find that lost paradise, he had to teach that child how to let go of trying to please a mother incapable of caring for him.

From his new role, Greg also could address the legitimate concerns of the worried six-year-old part of him by discovering that he could *choose* to start on small parts of his overwhelming project if he gave himself at least as much time to do the things he liked—guilt-free. Assuming the role of an effective coach, Greg chose a balanced work-life schedule that eased the part of him that needed to be the adaptive, good little boy while ensuring that the natural child had time for play.

As his inner conflict subsided, Greg systematically tackled small parts of his gigantic task, starting with fifteen minutes a day. He made sure that he didn't pressure himself and gave himself ample rewards for every uninterrupted period of work. Though it took almost a year, Greg finally completed all five years of his back taxes and legal forms—a task that initially seemed impossible.

Understanding, and empathizing with, the challenges you faced as a child can awaken the Self in you to offer both compassion and direction to the child you were and to the childhood memories still in you. In completing this process, you'll be equipped to provide—in the present—the acknowledgment and approval that child needed back then. With your guidance, it will no longer be stuck searching for unconditional acceptance in the past, in others who cannot give it, or in toxic, addictive substances.

Robert Bly, author of *Iron John*, has said: you may have been wounded as a child, but you are no longer the wounded child. *You* are the one who *has* a wounded child to care for, to protect, and to guide.

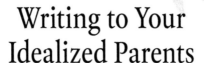

Writing to Your Idealized Parents

Grief is the sobbing and wailing that express the acceptance of our helplessness to do anything about losses. . . . [If we refuse to grieve,] then we are forever stuck with trying to redeem the past. [We] must learn to live well, in the present, beginning with things as they are. . . . if we refuse to accept the misfortunes of the past as unalterable, then we do not get to keep the warm, loving feelings intact.

—Sheldon Kopp, *Guru: Metaphors from a Psychotherapist*

Action Step Exercise: Writing Letters

This process moves you into the role of a mature, executive Self who accepts all your voices of doubt, fear, rebellion, worry, or lack of self-confidence and metabolizes and integrates them so you can move forward in your life with less struggle and with the full cooperation of every part of you.

Write two letters: one to your lost idealized childhood and one to your idealized parents. In these letters acknowledge your gratitude for the paradise of the first months of life. Appreciate that you most likely had some time in a state of blissful ease and paradise; otherwise you wouldn't keep searching for its return. Finally, mourn the loss of that time and the special relationship you had with the people who were, or tried to be, your ideal parents.

By preparing to mourn and bury the magical (but temporary) powers of childhood, you are stopping the frustrating search for the unconditional acceptance you once had from your idealized parents. Say goodbye to that Garden of Eden and to the parents who were there to give you, at least temporarily, the basic safety and love you needed.

Only then can you say to the part of you stuck in its search for an external paradise: "The struggle is over. There's no way to change the past. I must live in the real world of today—a world of human vulnerability and loss and change. Now you can let go of trying so hard to understand and fix the past. Come out of the past and help me move forward into my future."

Fear and Phobia

The fear of death follows from the fear of life. A man who lives fully is prepared to die at any time.

—Mark Twain

Practical solution.

Research and clinical practice over the last seventy years has shown that approaching the feared object safely and slowly helps decrease the strength of a phobic response. This method, developed by South African psychiatrist Dr. Joseph Wolpe, has been called *fear inoculation*, *systematic desensitization*, and *graduated exposure therapy.*

Systematic desensitization can begin with a mental rehearsal of gradually approaching the feared object (an insect, snake, dog) or situations (entering an airplane or elevator, hospitals, school exams). When the phobic reaction takes place, you stop the image or replace it with a calm, safe image. Once you experience lower reactivity, you can progress to the next level, for example, being in the same room with a spider, snake, or dog. You then systematically proceed up the hierarchy of fears until you can be relatively stress-free in the presence of the previously feared object or situation.

Imagery.

Imagine gradually approaching something you fear or avoid. When you are able to stay with the image for at least twenty to thirty seconds, the phobia will begin to lessen as your brain shifts from fight or flight (a lower-brain survival response), to higher-brain problem-solving and leadership. Imagine choosing to be near a feared object while breathing deeply and concentrating on your breathing. After approximately thirty seconds, shut off the scene and relax for one to two minutes before proceeding.

Imagine telling your fearful brain: "I've got this. I'm choosing to overcome my phobia by systematically approaching it, staying with it for three to six deep breaths, as my stress response subsides, and I realize that I'm safe and still alive."

Putting it to use.

Those who are the most fearful and stressed tend to use self-criticism and even self-hating language when talking to themselves. Those with minimal fear and stress talk to themselves with compassionate and self-accepting words and thoughts.

To help phobic or fearful clients lower their stress, I often ask, "What will you say to yourself in the last moments of life?" Think about it. Will you be cursing yourself or accusing yourself of making a stupid mistake? Or will you be at peace with your life and your human vulnerability? The answer to that question tells your body and mind to feel safe with you or to fear you.

Prepare what you will say to yourself in the last moments of your life. How calm and safe will you feel if you make an agreement with yourself that says, "In the last moments of my life I will be curious, interested, and accepting. I will be at peace with my life and grateful. Thank you for this life."

Fear of Death: Knowing What You'll Say to Yourself in Your Last Moments

My aerial surveillance team in Vietnam was part of the 101st Airborne's advanced intelligence unit. We had our technical work of interpreting aerial photos and heat-sensing imagery in support of the combat units, but we didn't engage the Vietcong directly. So most of our days in Vietnam were relatively quiet.

The boredom and quiet was violently broken on the unusually noisy day I learned what I will say to myself in my last moments: "Be still, and watch what happens. This is going to be interesting."

That day was relatively peaceful until midmorning, when I heard and felt the shock of multiple explosions uncomfortably close to my tent. Mortars had hit our ammo dump, exploding a series of shells and shaking the earth. I immediately dove for the nearest foxhole as the explosions continued from twenty yards away. A second later my sergeant jumped in, covering his ears and bracing, as I was, for the next blast. We each saw tears in the other man's eyes; but we weren't crying—it was tear gas! The first few Vietcong mortars had hit the tear gas canisters, and not the highly explosive 155-mm artillery shells! We had gotten a reprieve. We both knew, simultaneously, that we had a few more seconds to climb out of our foxhole and race from the ammo dump to the opposite end of camp near the landing strip.

As I remember that experience, it's all happening in slow motion, seeming to take somewhere between ten seconds and thirty minutes. I expected to feel stress and fear, but what was running through my mind was a weird curiosity about how I was going to die. Would it be from an explosion that ruptured blood vessels in my brain? Would a ball of fire pull the air from my lungs and burn me? Would I feel pain? I was experiencing a crazy curiosity, not fear! I thought, how weird: I'm not afraid; I'm just curious! When my time comes, I'll probably be curious about what that transition will be like. The events of that day have stayed with me and have lessened my fear of death.

I have had clients in therapy who were in the last months or days of their lives. To my surprise, most were not afraid of dying, but they were afraid of a painful death, of leaving loved ones behind and losing control over how they die. This is one of the top fears that people have. When asked, "What's the worst that could happen?" most people answer, "I could die."

That's why I'd like to suggest that you prepare what you would say to yourself in the last moments of your life as a way to lessen many of your fears. It's a contract between the conscious *you* and your body and subconscious mind that offers inner peace and acceptance, regardless of what happens.

It's a courageous and empowering practice to consider what you will say to yourself and how you will treat yourself in the last moments of your life. This could lessen your fear of death along with other fears.

Nine years after my tour in Vietnam, I was in a cancer ward, diagnosed with terminal cancer. The doctor told me I had one year to live. I knew I could die; I wasn't in denial about that. But I wasn't going to be scared into treatments that didn't make sense or let myself be pressured into surgery until I had a second and a third opinion. I simply thought, *this is going to be an interesting year.*

I asked my doctor what research he was basing his treatment plan on. Obviously unhappy with my questions, he impatiently said, "Most people are afraid of dying, including me." I gathered that this meant, "Just follow orders and stop asking dumb questions."

I replied from some place deep inside me, "I'm not afraid of dying, but I am afraid of what your fear of cancer could do to me." He didn't know that I had faced the possibility of death several times earlier in my life and that I knew I would not be afraid. I knew I could count on every part of me to be curious about this last moment without complaint or self-criticism. I knew I would not be cursing myself or making myself feel miserable. I am as certain as a human can be that I will be grateful for my life and for the gift of inner peace in my last moments. I trust that I will maintain my commitment to myself: "I'm on your side. Regardless of what happens, I accept you. Your worth is safe with me."

Turning Down the Pilot Light on My Life

Eight years after surviving cancer, I started to train for a marathon. As if to challenge the bravado of that previous experience, life taught me a lesson in the form of a humbling, exhausting attack of pneumonia. I was running at least five miles a day, six days a week, ignoring signs that I was coming down with a bad cold or flu. I continued to ignore my body's messages to rest and as a result turned a flu into pneumonia.

Having pneumonia felt as if someone were turning down the pilot light on my life. I was so exhausted but I was afraid to fall asleep, because I didn't know if I'd wake up. Even when the medication began to work, I had to sleep for sixteen or more hours a day.

Each time I started to fall asleep, I was confronted with the fear of not waking up. In spite of what I had learned in Vietnam and during my experience with cancer, I *was* afraid of dying. I had escaped several near-death experiences, and now I had a real feeling of what dying might feel like—the slow turning down of my breath and the pilot light of my life. Several times a day I faced that fear and a colossal choice: struggle to stay awake or risk the possibility of dying in my sleep.

Pneumonia served as a tangible test—more so than jumping out of airplanes, explosions in the ammo dump, or facing cancer—of my ability to confront my fear of death. It gave me the opportunity to bring forth the human courage it takes to accept the reality of impermanence.

Hopefully, in my last moments, I will remember to say: "Be still and watch what happens. This is going to be interesting."

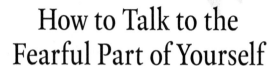

How to Talk to the Fearful Part of Yourself

How you talk to yourself will determine if you experience inner peace or fear.

- ❧ Practice starting with "yes" to acknowledge the fears and concerns of those parts of you that, for survival reasons, are naturally sensitive to danger and fear.

- ❧ Avoid saying "It's OK." The fearful part of us knows it's not OK.

- ❧ Demonstrate compassionate leadership. When you start showing up as the leader in your life, all parts will relax and contribute to your mission.

In these examples of what you can say to the fearful part of you, notice the use of "yes . . . and."

"*Yes*, I see your fears, *and* they are valid and normal."

"*Yes*, you've been trying to solve problems on your own, *and* now you don't have to; I'm here with you. A part of you knows how to be in this world in a more robust, easy, and joyful way."

"*Yes*, that *was* very painful. There is nothing wrong with you, except that you are human. *And* I accept your humanness. You will not be abandoned by life or me because of your pain and loss. Though you don't how, you will survive, just as you learned to stand, walk, and ride a bike, even though you didn't know how."

"*Yes*, you don't know how to do it all, *and* now, I'm choosing to show up, focus on starting, and go from not knowing to knowing. Fear and lack of confidence can't stop our commitment to this mission."

Write down how you will talk to yourself in your own words, using the "Yes . . . and" construction.

_____

_____

_____

_____

_____

_____

_____

_____

_____

Coping with Cancer

I used to make choices using only my intellect. Now I have many more ways of making choices because I now listen to my body, to my heart, to my intuition. . . . I remain an agnostic. . . . But I am clear about the human need to surrender to something bigger. To live a complete life, I need something larger than my intellect.

—TONY SCHWARTZ, *What Really Matters*

Before I was diagnosed with terminal cancer at the age of thirty-two and given one year to live, I thought my feelings, behaviors, and patterns were unchangeable parts of who I was. For example, I was self-righteous about my smoking, my tendency to work without stopping, my impatience, and my aggressive driving. When my fiancée would ask me to change these habits, I would become defensive and argue that she was asking me to change my personality.

After my cancer diagnosis, I began to see that my reactions, thoughts, and habits had to change if I was to have the best possible chance of living to see thirty-three. My new attitude and habits would have to be strong enough to survive a journey that included surgery, innumerable medical tests, eighteen months of chemotherapy, and possibly radiation.

I was given a 10 percent chance to live one year, so the odds were clearly against me. I told myself, "If I can't beat the odds, I'm going to make this a very interesting year. I'm not going to waste what might be the last year of my life in fear, passively following doctor's orders or making myself feel bad."

With fierce determination, I took on a protective role toward my time, my body, and my life. After I fired my first surgeon, I met with three others before agreeing to exploratory surgery to determine if my tumor was cancerous.

Once surgery confirmed that I did have cancer and that surgery had been necessary to make a definitive diagnosis, I felt a strange sense of relief. I realized that if I had made a mistake by agreeing to have surgery when there was no cancer, some part of me would be furious and make me feel miserable. I was shocked to discover that I was afraid of incurring my own wrath for not making a perfect decision!

Getting Your Dictator to Cooperate

I named this part of me the "dictator." This dictator part would need to be integrated into my larger Self if I was going to maintain some remnant of inner peace during the months of chemotherapy that lay before me. I started to make my choices very carefully and consciously. To ensure that they truly were *choices* and not shoulds or have-tos, I would tell myself, "You *don't have to* do this. I can live with the consequences either way. I won't let the dictator make you feel bad."

As I awakened to playing a leadership role in my life, my sense of mission and values became clearer. If I were going to maximize my chances of survival, every part of me needed to be aligned with that mission and those values. Every part of me—even the dictator—needed to commit to my vision of living in inner peace, with minimal stress and unambivalent action for whatever time I had left.

Uniting All Parts

If you don't know where you're going, you'll probably end up someplace else.   —Yogi Berra

Following surgery to remove the cancerous tumor, I found a doctor who agreed with me that chemotherapy, rather than more surgery, made sense in my case. He told me that I needed weekly doses of a very strong chemotherapy cocktail for nine months, and monthly doses for another year or so to ensure that this very virulent cancer was eradicated from my body. With chemotherapy taking a large toll on my energy, I had to choose my fights and what to get upset about if I expected to continue working, tolerate the full treatment, go out in the evening, or have energy to write about my cancer experience.

It was this longer fight that taught me the most about the qualities necessary for uniting all parts of myself around my objectives and values. Many times I caught myself hoping that I could surrender responsibility for my life to a doctor who wanted to play God and take charge. But the larger wisdom I needed to surrender to wasn't in a doctor or a miracle cure. I needed to believe in a larger sense of Self within me—something larger than my intellect that could unite the wisdom of my mind, body, and intuition.

After the first nine months, the schedule of chemotherapy treatments changed from weekly to monthly, and only then could I experience their real effects on my body. After each chemotherapy treatment, I felt as if I had the flu or pneumonia for two weeks. Then my energy would return so that I could even jog a few miles before having another treatment and beginning the cycle over again. I rode this emotional and physical roller-coaster for nine more months before asking my doctor, "What if I stop the chemo now?" He answered that I should continue chemotherapy for at least six to nine more months. But since I had lived for eighteen months beyond the diagnosis, the odds had reversed, and there was now a 90 percent chance that I was cured.

That evening, I sat in my living room with a pen and a pad and convened a "committee meeting" of all my inner voices. I closed my eyes, turned my head down as if looking inward, and told every part of me that I was about to end chemotherapy unless the doctor could convince me to continue. I considered what I had asked my body to go through for eighteen months, and I weighed the risks of stopping chemotherapy against the recommendations of my doctor and the experts.

I realized that, to be true to myself, I couldn't stop treatment just because some part of me didn't want the pain and disruption chemotherapy caused me. I knew that I couldn't continue just because some part of me was afraid of making a mistake by not following orders. Regardless of which direction I chose, I knew every part of me would have to be committed to the mission.

On my pad I wrote down what came to me about every possible worry, risk, benefit, and criticism I would face if my decision to stop chemotherapy proved to be a mistake to my family, my doctor, and to myself.

I imagined each scenario and acknowledged each "What if. . . ?" and each "What if the cancer comes back?" Most frequently, I responded with, "Yes, that would be awful. Yes, that would really hurt. Yes, I'd probably cry and be upset. And I won't let it last for long. I am taking full responsibility for this decision. I can live with the consequences."

During that committee meeting, I realized that the dictator part of me that had revealed itself at the time of my surgery a year and a half earlier had truly been integrated into my larger Self. Now there was barely any fear of making a mistake; it became clear that *I*—in the role of my leadership Self—was in charge and could minimize the self-criticism if the cancer came back or if some inner voice said, "See, I told you so. You acted on your own, and you made a big mistake."

The dictator and his self-righteous voice were gone or had been transformed into a helpful member of my team. And *I* certainly was transformed, over those eighteen months of chemotherapy, into the one who was now in charge of his life. That night, seated in the chairperson's role for almost an hour, I reached a new level of integration—a sense of a Self that was whole. It was both calming and empowering to feel that I had a complete team behind my decision to stop chemotherapy.

At our next appointment, the doctor tested my resolve, saying, "I'm responsible for your life. You don't need to make these kinds of decisions." Two years earlier, I would have prayed for someone or something outside of me to take responsibility for my life, but now I was speaking up for every part of me. I was in a leadership role and was empowered to tell the doctor with conviction, "I will consider your advice, doctor, but only *I* can be responsible for my life. After all, I'm the one who will live or die with the consequences of these decisions."

I ended chemotherapy that day and have lived to tell about it at the hospital's grand rounds and in my article for *The New England Journal of Medicine*. This was not a cavalier decision. I already had surgery and had withstood nine months of weekly chemotherapeutic agents and another nine months of monthly treatments. That chemotherapy saved my life. But it was time to give my body a chance to heal and clean up any remnants of cancer cells with its own resources.

Not many patients *choose* to take chemotherapy, much less demand it. My case may be unusual, but it does demonstrate that patients can participate in their healthcare, even in the treatment of cancer.

Habit Change

Practical solution.

Habits, such as brushing your teeth or preparing coffee or tea in the morning, make it easier to do routine tasks without having to think about them or to decide *if* you're going to do them. Habits move you effortlessly through the numerous steps of a complex activity such as driving your car, riding a bike, playing the piano or guitar. After weeks, months, and years of repetition, you automatically proceed through the phases without much effort or thought because you have developed an automatic link between steps that we call a habit.

This makes well-ingrained habits difficult to change when they no longer fit your current situation, health issues, or goals. Americans driving a car in England, for example, must be very mindful of staying to the left side of the road rather than relying on their habit of driving on the right side. A long-term habit of smoking or eating sugar may need to stop for health reasons. How will you do it? What makes changing a habit difficult for you?

Imagery.

Imagine you're anticipating a stressful work environment and you know you could be tempted to regress to old habits such as overeating, smoking, or depending on an abusive relative. Your self-soothing old habits can appear first as simply thoughts ("I could use a smoke or a drink right about now"), and, if not stopped or replaced, will lead to an urge or compulsion ("I've got to have something to take the edge off"). It's easier to catch and replace a habit at the thought stage, but it is still possible to move to a corrective action if you've reached the impulsive stage.

Your chances of being successful in changing negative habits are greater when you plan ahead, anticipating the thought and the urge, and have a corrective action to replace them.

Putting it to use.

Linking the old habit to a new direction is one of the fastest ways to change or break a habit. Breaking a negative habit involves linking the old tendency, or subconscious *reaction*, to the consciously *chosen* corrective action that leads to achieving your new goal.

To be most effective, you'll want to try making "if-then" plans to replace bad habits with good. You'll want to move from offtrack to back on track and to shift from negative thought or impulse to your higher mission, from dissociated parts of you to your integrated higher Self.

In her book, *Succeed: How We Can Reach Our Goals*, Heidi Grant Halvorson, PhD, writes that if-then plans can more than double your chances of succeeding in overcoming negative habits. Over a hundred studies have shown that deciding in advance what you will do if the old habit arises (for example, "*If* I'm hungry and thinking about eating candy") leads to success when followed with a planned "*then I will*" (for example: "*Then I will* eat a piece of fruit).

A generic plan to replace a habitual, "*if I*" am going down the old path, could be "*then I will* take a few deep breaths." You can apply "take a few breaths" in many situations to follow an "*If I*"—for example, get bored, angry, tired, jealous. Most habitual reactions will subside within ten to fifteen seconds (that's two to three breaths) if you refuse to follow the usual habit down the old path. That's just enough time for you to apply your planned "*then I will*," and you're on your way to replacing an outdated negative habit with one that is aligned with your current values and goals.

Hot tip.

Develop a compelling, magnetic vision that pulls you in from habits that distract you from the path to your goals. Empower your higher Self to protect your body, your life, and your career from negative habits. You'll learn that you don't have to be controlled by old habits or distracting thoughts and feelings. For example, I still have thoughts about smoking a cigarette, even though I stopped smoking over forty years ago. But thoughts and even cravings—regardless of how strong they may be—can't control how I *choose* to act when I have such a solid commitment to protect my body from tobacco, old habits, and addictions. Now I can observe the thought, and even the impulse, of smoking with great curiosity and compassion. Instead of something I feel compelled to do, these thoughts and feeling are simply outdated reactions that remind my strongest Self to keep its commitment to the mission of protecting my body and my life.

Changing Your Default

When you have established a clear, compelling mission, you can more quickly identify your old habits (or "defaults") as deviations and rapidly self-correct, get back on track, and refocus on productive action.

By linking awareness of your default reactions to corrective action, you'll become incredibly efficient and effective at limiting the destructive effects of the five major problem areas: stress, inner conflict, self-criticism, feeling overwhelmed, and struggle.

My default speed when driving on city streets where the speed limit is 25 mph is 42 mph. How do I know this? In the past I was clocked by the police three times doing 42 mph—that's 17 mph over the posted speed limit—and carries a hefty fine. If I don't pay attention or get lost listening to music, my automatic habit would most likely get me another ticket for going 42 mph.

So how did I get out of this expensive, and dangerous, habit? I now *acknowledge my default* and I link it to my consciously chosen speed of 25 mph and my commitment to obey the speed limit.

These strategies have helped me change an automatic, subconscious default behavior by noticing it, recalling the pain and expense it has caused me, and linking it to a consciously chosen corrective action and value. My driving is now more aligned with my higher values and mission. You'll be more in charge of your reactive habits as you consciously choose to act in ways congruent with your values and goals.

Do Your Habits Contribute to Your Mission or Detract?

Clarity of *mission* makes it easier to stay on course and to minimize diversions that might too easily waste precious time and energy.

—Neil Fiore, *Coping with the Emotional Aspects of Cancer*

When I was undergoing nine months of weekly chemotherapy, the first thing I told myself was, "The cancer didn't simply spread to my lung; it's being *held* there by my lung's ability to filter debris from the bloodstream. My body is an active ally, not a passive victim. I want to do what I can to help the healthy part of me fight cancer and cooperate with the medication."

I began to see that certain thoughts and actions clearly contributed to feeling alive in the moment, and other thoughts distracted me from my mission of living as fully as I could for as long as I could. My life became very simple, thanks to a famous line in Shakespeare's *Hamlet*. When deciding what to do, I would ask myself repeatedly, "To be, or not to be? Does this thought or action contribute to my health, well-being, and being fully alive, or does it detract?"

Because my top priorities, mission, and role as protector of my time, body, and life were so clear, it took me only seconds to decide how to act. This laserlike focus helped me instantly let go of negative thoughts and focus on my mission, path, and higher values. In carrying out my commitment to myself, at times I'd respond to a request from my friends and family with, "No thank you; that sounds like work." Telemarketers heard, "No thank you; I don't have the time." And when you've been given a terminal cancer diagnosis, you can say, "I don't have the time" with true conviction.

Examples of Mission Statements

To help you create an overarching sense of mission, I've listed my mission statements and vision as examples. (Note that *I* means "my strongest Self" in its leadership and protective roles.)

❧ *I* am committed to accepting reality rather than fighting against it. Life and other people are not a problem or enemies, but simply facts.

❧ *I* limit my stress reaction to less than thirty seconds. Self-threats are no longer acceptable. *I* communicate to every part of me, "Your worth is safe with me. Regardless of what happens, *I* will not make you feel bad."

❧ *I* manage my life from *choice* rather than from the ambivalence that's caused by the inner conflict between "You have to" and "I don't want to." Ambivalence and inner conflict now wake up my strongest Self to make an executive choice.

❧ *I* rapidly move from an isolated, worrying conscious mind and shift it to wondering what the deeper wisdom of my larger, integrated mind and body will achieve.

❧ *I* take at least three deep breaths before starting to work in order to connect with a deeper system of support, to link my left brain with my right brain, and to connect with the wisdom of my body.

❧ *I* integrate every part of me into a powerful, focused team. No single part of me works alone or carries full responsibility for my life.

❧ *I*, as my strongest Self, am in charge of my life, not the six-year-old or the two-year-old or any part of my lower brain. From the perspective of my integrated, higher Self, *I* take responsibility for my life and the role of guiding all parts of me toward my higher values and mission.

Write your own mission statements and commitments to yourself.

❧ _____

_____

❧ _____

_____

❧ _____

_____

Visualize Your Mission: A Path to Corrective Action

When you develop a compelling mission, you'll have a powerful tool to help you achieve your goals and realize your true potential more quickly and efficiently. The more clearly you can define your *chosen* life mission, the sooner you'll be able to shift from default *reactions* and redirect your attention to the *chosen* action that leads to inner peace, optimal performance, and success.

You'll be able to respond to old obstacles, challenges, and problems in just seconds, replacing them with the qualities of your strongest Self.

Think of your higher values, qualities, and vision (for example, feeling internally peaceful, stress-free, focused, and committed) as a compelling magnetic path or lane that pulls you in from your distractions and old, outdated ways of coping.

You might use the imagery of driving on a rainy highway to practice focusing on your lane or path in spite of anger at oncoming high beams and trucks spraying water across your windshield. Link distracting thoughts and old habits to the corrective action of getting back on track and back to your mission, staying in your lane and leading yourself safely to your destination.

Under pressure at work or in competitive sports, you don't have time to waste getting angry or scared: you refocus on your objective, exhaling (as with a karate shout) and releasing tension in less than two seconds as you concentrate on your mission and higher values. Practice refocusing on corrective action, and you will more consistently achieve the optimal performance of a champion who stays *in the zone, the groove,* or *flow state* that is far beyond your usual level of play. (See part II, *Beyond Practical Solutions,* for suggestions on how to perform optimally in the zone.)

Effective Communication Skills

Relationships of all kinds—business, professional, and personal—rely on respectful and clear communication. One of the most practical solutions to a multitude of issues is effective communications.

Practical solution.

Listen so intensely that you can repeat almost verbatim what the other person is saying. Check in to ensure your understanding is correct. For example: "If I understand you correctly, you're really upset with me for not calling you last night." "I embarrassed you. Is that right?" "You're saying you don't feel appreciated; am I understanding you correctly?"

Demonstrate that you're interested in understanding the other's thoughts, feelings, perspective, and experience as opposed to trying to win a debate, defending yourself, or acting like a cheerleader. Avoid arguing, debating, or being overly positive in the face of the other's pain.

Imagery.

Set a scene: one person is talking (this could be your partner, customer, or coworker), and you are looking at your cell phone. The speaker becomes angry with you. What do you do? What do you say? Remember, avoid arguing or being defensive. Demonstrate that you're interested in understanding the other's point of view and feelings, not trying to fix them or argue away their feelings.

Putting it to use.

Practice using these tools and guidelines:

- ❧ Find a way to say "Yes, and" and "Yes, of course" rather than "No, that's crazy."
- ❧ Attempt to understand the other's point of view rather than arguing from yours. For example: "Yes, I apologize. I was distracted by a text I've been waiting for. Please tell me again what you were saying."
- ❧ Avoid arguing. Make this a win-win situation. Your goal is to *understand* and to *demonstrate* that you're interested in your partner's feelings and perspective.
- ❧ Demonstrate that you respect the feelings and experience of your partner. Even when you disagree with their opinion, attempt to learn something.

- Demonstrate that you are an ally, not a threat, a problem, or an enemy. Use *I* statements ("I have a problem. I'm sensitive about . . . so when you . . . I get upset, hurt, angry") as opposed to "you are too controlling."

- Stick to your subjective truth, your problem, and what you would like to achieve as opposed to "You should . . ." or "You always . . ." For example, "I get defensive when I'm blamed. I can listen better when you tell me what I'm doing right or what you want rather than accusing me of not caring about how you feel."

- Avoid ultimatums, mind reading, analyzing, absolutes, universals, and dictating to the other, for example, "You should stop being so negative. You're *always* late, *always* forgetting."

- Avoid sarcasm or kidding during a serious discussion. Acknowledge your hurt or anger directly with an assertive *I* statement rather than sarcasm.

- Avoid the role of a fixer, rescuer, or superior know-it-all played to the other's role of student, servant, and grateful receiver of your help, beneficence, and wisdom. Your well-intentioned help will be seen as insulting and will be resisted, and you will feel unappreciated. Demonstrate instead that you are another vulnerable human being, with limited control and, unfortunately, limited power to solve all their problems or heal all wounds. Repeat to yourself: "I am not your problem, not your enemy and, unfortunately, not your solution."

🍃 Try saying "That's not like you" when someone acts in a way that is not acceptable. This gives them a moment to shift to their higher Self—the one you're waiting to engage. Don't waste time with their lesser egos. Understand that the other's initial harsh reactions may be old protective devices that obscure the true person hiding beneath the crusty exterior. "That's not like you" tells them that you remember their better, more enlightened self: the one that you expect from them.

🍃 Avoid cross-complaining, arguing, or debating. Stick with the current feelings. Communication is most effective when focused on one speaker or issue at a time. This requires *nondefensive listening*. The initiator of a complaint or issue needs to be (1) heard, (2) understood, and (3) satisfied that an agreement addresses the issue.

🍃 Do not analyze why the other person is feeling upset or require that they be perfect before they can express their feelings. This is not the time to return a question with a question such as, "Why are you so sensitive?"

🍃 Stop avoiding the feelings. Don't turn this into an intellectual debate. When you can't convince the other, attempt to build rapport and mutual respect.

- Schedule cooldown periods when arguments become circular. Agree upon a time to talk after cooling down. For example: "Is this a good time for you to talk? Would tonight at nine be better?"

- Think, act, and communicate from the principle, "I am not your enemy, problem, or solution. *I am simply a fact* (as are you)." Refuse to pick up the end of a rope offered as a tug-of-war. Refuse to be the enemy or the solution for your partner or children. Instead communicate that "you may be having a problem with life or someone from your past. Please take a walk or go to your room to work it out. I'll be here when you're ready to accept my love and support."

Hot tip.

Mourn the loss of your ideal childhood and unconditional acceptance in order to stop the frustrating search for the ideal partner or ideal family (it doesn't exist) and the fantasy of finding an external fix to all your problems.

Letting go of the struggle to keep the past alive completes the mourning process and frees you to live fully in the reality of today—the reality of this relationship.

Part II
Beyond Practical
Solutions

Digging Deeper

Shifting from Limited Identity to True Self

The human mind ... [is born into a] collective conditioning ... that is total delusion. ... But to see the conditioning in oneself is to begin to get free of it. Then you
wonder what part of you sees this? That seeing part's
ability to observe the workings of the mind is a new
level of consciousness arising, a new level of awareness:
to see one's conditioning and observe it in action ...
then comes the choice not to identify with those mental
structures.   —ECKHART TOLLE, *The Power of Now*

The following concepts about how the human brain
functions are offered in the hope that they will inspire
you to choose how to act from your higher human brain
rather than reacting from your lower animal brain. Your

brain has evolved over millions of years and contains the equivalent of the whole brain of an alligator, a horse, and an ape, as well as a part that makes you distinctly human. This chapter can prepare you to use more of your brain cell capacity as you assume the role of a wise and compassionate leader of your own self and your life.

The newest brain on the planet—some anthropologists say it's less than 200,000 years old—is the part of our brain that makes us human. It's located primarily in the forehead as an enhancement of three lower brains: the reptilian, fight-or-flight brain; the mammal bonding brain; and the primate toolmaker brain. In addition, we have left- and right-brain hemispheres, which specialize in separate functions. With a brain composed of so many parts and levels, we humans need a function that's in charge of managing, overriding, and directing lower, more primitive brains. That's where the Self and its leadership "new brain" come in.

The new vertical forehead, containing our human executive and leadership functions, underwent a major change in consciousness that coincides with the end of the last Ice Age 11,700 years ago. Humans, who had been mostly hunters, gatherers, and scavengers who followed animal migrations, became farmers and shepherds who settled in one place and built homes and villages. For millions of years, early humans spent a large part of each day gathering plants and hunting or scavenging animals. In the last 12,000 years, modern humans (*Homo sapiens*) have made the transition to growing crops and domesticating animals such as oxen, horses, sheep, pigs, and dogs. This shift caused a major transformation in our brains, our species, and the planet.

This relatively rapid change in behavior implies a massive leap in the evolution of consciousness. It is most likely a contributing factor in the advent of "self-conscious" consciousness and an awareness of self as separate from others.

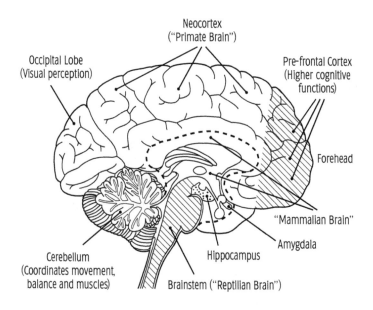

In this diagram, notice that the prefrontal cortex is in the forward part of the primate brain and somewhat higher than the reptilian brain stem and the mammal brain.

Identifying as an individual, separate from others and the tribe, is relatively new in human history. According to Julian Jaynes, author of *The Origin of Consciousness in the Breakdown of the Bicameral Mind* (1976), consciousness—the human ability to introspect and maintain a separate sense of self—evolved in the last four thousand years. This is relevant to our study of practical solutions because these recent changes in climate, human behavior, and culture also brought about something we take for granted today: the sense of a separate self or limited identity. In this next section, I attempt to offer several exercises to help you shift from a limited, separate sense of self—sometimes called *ego identity*—to a truer, more complete and integrated Self.

You Don't Have to Struggle beside Yourself

We are dominated by everything with which our (ego) becomes identified. We can dominate and control everything from which we dis-identify ourselves.

—Roberto Assagioli, *Psychosynthesis*

Keeping your identify stuck in a small, outdated part of who you truly are limits your capabilities to what you knew and could do as a child. You'll be stuck in the past, separated from your larger, wiser, and stronger Self. From its limited resources, your old identity (or ego identity or persona) will try hard to manage your life. This makes you more vulnerable to stress, worry, self-doubt, confusion, and fear of criticism and rejection. It's exhausting to work so hard as if you're alone and separate from a larger system of support within yourself and your community.

Trying to cope with life while disconnected from a larger support system makes you vulnerable to seeking escape through external fixes to ease the pain. Those disconnected from a larger sense of self and a larger support system tend to seek comfort through addictive behaviors such as overeating, abuse of alcohol, drugs, and excessive TV watching or obsessively surfing the Internet.

Shifting your identity to a more expansive Self, on the other hand, decreases stress, self-sabotage, and your dependency on drugs or unhealthy relationships. It also increases your capacity for creativity and productivity by uniting your conscious mind with your subconscious mind, and the left-brain hemisphere with the right.

To learn how the process of connecting to a larger Self is radically different from simply pressuring your ego, "lesser parts," or personality to try harder, you'll want to perform a little experiment.

Complete this exercise if you wish to benefit fully from this process.

Essential Exercise: Separate or Connected

STEP 1. Hold a book, briefcase, or purse straight out at shoulder height in one hand until you feel uncomfortable or tired. Imagine doing this all day, every day, every week, and consider what habits and dependencies you would develop in order to simply cope with the pain and survive.

STEP 2. Once again, hold the object out in front of you until you feel tired. Then bring your elbow to your hip or side (some call this the *core* or *the place of chi*). Now place your other hand underneath the object to support the object's weight. Notice how much easier it is to hold the same weight when your arm is connected to the rest of your body and to the support of your opposite hand.

For an even greater sense of connection with something beyond your isolated, struggling arm (representing your separated ego identity), stand and bend your knees, consciously letting your hips, legs, and feet sink into the support of the floor.

Take a deep breath, hold it, and as you exhale, imagine that you're floating down into the support of the floor, the building, and the earth itself. Your ego, personality, and conscious mind are no longer working and struggling alone. You now are connected to the larger, wiser support system in your body, your mind, and the laws of nature that hold you.

The discomfort you felt in the first part of this exercise is analogous to the struggle, fatigue, and pain that you may feel in life when a part of you—represented in this exercise by your extended arm and hand—acts as if it must work alone, separate from any support. By performing this simple exercise, you learn that everything is easier when you connect your ego and conscious mind to the larger support system of your Self and whole brain (represented in this exercise by your body and its connection to the floor and the earth.)

When you expand your identity beyond the isolated, lesser parts of your personality and ego identity, you integrate your conscious and subconscious resources, making it easier to face life's challenges from a center of inner peace and greater support. The same can be said when you expand your resources to include friends and a community that validate your worth and create an environment in which you are safe to be your true Self.

The world-famous psychiatrist and clinical hypnotist Dr. Milton H. Erickson used to say that much of our fear about life comes from thinking of ourselves as if we were a small cup of water. From that limited perspective, the loss of just a few drops of water would feel like a serious threat to our identity and security. To paraphrase Dr. Erickson: If you think of yourself as a small cup of water, you'll be afraid of losing just a few drops. How different it is to be the ocean! When you're the ocean, they can take a cup or a whole tub of water from you, and it won't hurt you one bit.

Many of our former problems and symptoms diminish when we learn to live from our larger, oceanic Self.

Choose Your True Self or a Separated, Limited Identity*

The fastest way to change is to change who you think
you are—to change your identity

—NEIL FIORE, PhD, *Awaken Your Strongest Self*

Look at the table on the next pages. Notice which symptoms of the separated, lonely, struggling ego in the column on the right best describe your current behavior
patterns. Then study the qualities in the column on the
left that you'll be gaining as you learn to connect with
and live from your Strongest Self.

Whenever you notice that your thoughts and feelings (outlined in the right-hand column) are similar to

* Adapted from Neil Fiore, *Awaken Your Strongest Self* (New York:
McGraw-Hill, 2010)

those of someone struggling from a limited sense of themselves, quickly shift to the behaviors, actions, and thoughts of someone living from their truer, stronger Self (as in the left-hand column).

Truer Self: Connected	Limited Identity: Separated, Lonely
Mourn the loss of paradise, unlimited power, and unconditional love	Deny their loss; maintain the illusion of unlimited power; feel guilty, codependent
Acknowledge and accept their vulnerability to suffering and loss	Deny their vulnerability and become extremely anxious about potential loss
Are self-accepting and forgiving; provide safety from threats, thereby minimizing stress	Are self-critical; frequently use self-threatening statements that cause chronic stress
Have a clear vision and priorities that keep them congruent with their higher values	Are distracted by latest urgency; are always working for some imagined future security
Give themselves inner worth, safe from judgment	Determine their worth by external events, others, and their own performance
Have access to inner resources that allow them to perform optimally with ease	Struggle because they rely solely on the limited resources of their conscious mind and nervous system
Operate from choice, thereby breaking inner conflict between parts to support their leadership mission	Remain immobilized and ambivalent because of the inner conflict between the inner voices of "have to" versus "I don't want to"

Truer Self: Connected	Limited Identity: Separated, Lonely
Can enjoy the present as a precious moment of life	Are anxious about the future and regretful about the past
Work from a win-win perspective that builds relationships and allows for different points of view	Operate from win-lose, right-wrong thinking that creates arguments and conflict
Connect with the deeper wisdom and support of their stronger Self, allowing spontaneity and relaxation	Need to control outcomes and stay vigilant in order to avoid mistakes and maintain an illusion of security

The Actor's Exercise: Changing Roles, Changing Identities

Shifting from a small, struggling, part of yourself to a grounded, integrated, stronger Self is a practical solution that resolves many issues by changing or expanding your identity. This shift will enhance your performance in several fields. The following actor's exercise is one way to shift out of an old, limited identity, freeing you to access your greater wisdom, strength and abilities.

Purpose of the Actor's Exercise

This exercise can help you change roles, perspectives, and moods the way you might if you were an actor moving from one play or movie to another. It can also make you aware of your ability to choose roles that quickly shift your sense of self out of negative, outdated roles and feelings.

When you (or an actor) are playing a particular role, you may identify completely with that role, feeling that it's truly who you are, but it's only your temporary identity. It's just like a suit of clothes that you can put on and take off, depending on the event, be it business, sports, or formal. Inside that new outfit, you feel like a new person, a different version of some essential you. The Self inside that role or suit remains the same. The characters you play in your dreams are all parts of you and are aspects of your same, essential Self.

Your first role. Imagine that you're an actor who's been playing the part of a depressed, down-and-out person for over a year. From the first moment you wearily haul yourself on stage, before you say one word, the audience knows that you're depressed and feel hopeless. They see you dragging your feet as you slink across the stage, shoulders bowed, head hung low, as if you're carrying a heavy burden on your shoulders. You speak to yourself in the voice of someone who's been depressed for decades.

You've played the role so many times that it's hard for you to shift out of the role and back to your usual self. It's as if the depressed character in the play has taken over your life. You've become so good at embodying your character that even the other actors and your friends have begun to think of you as depressed.

PROBLEM. The play is closing tonight and you must prepare for a new role.

Your second role. Tomorrow you audition for the role of a very successful, confident person who has always known ease and comfort, and who effortlessly surmounts the greatest of difficulties. In this role, you are the exact opposite of your former depressed role. The way you enter a room, greet others, and are alert to the beauty in the world all signal that you're very much alive and comfortable with yourself. It wouldn't matter if you were fifty pounds overweight or had a severe handicap; in this role, you have charisma and confidence. People are glad to see you because your joy at simply being alive is infectious and generously shared. They greet you the way a grandparent greets a beloved grandchild or the way a fan looks up to film star or an athlete.

PHYSICAL CHANGE. Notice how you must change your body and posture in order to shift from the depressed role to the joyful, energized role. Experiment with trying to have a depressing thought and feeling while you hold your head up, keep your shoulders back, and put a smile on your face. Write down your observations.

_____

_____

_____

_____

EMOTIONAL CHANGE. Notice how your feelings change as you let go of the depressive history and take on the history and script of a successful, confident person. Notice the change from fatigue and low motivation to high energy as you shift to a view of a life with possibilities and with the inner resources to confront challenges. Write down what your experience.

_____

_____

_____

_____

INNER DIALOGUE CHANGE. Notice how differently you talk to yourself in the role of a depressed character as opposed to the supportive, encouraging inner dialogue of a joyful person. Make up some thoughts and words of self-support that would fit the inner dialogue of cheerful, effective, hopeful persons. Practice the walk, gestures, and inner dialogue of someone who has faced many challenges and has persevered because of inner safety and self-support. How would they talk to themselves after a loss or failure? What inner dialogue would help them to recover from a tragedy and move on with their lives? Write down your thoughts and your new inner dialogue.

_____

_____

_____

_____

Change Your Identity to Get into the Zone

Most of our problems come from thinking of ourselves as a separate, struggling, outdated ego identity. Most of our solutions come from connecting to a larger sense of Self, connected to and supported by the wisdom of our complete brain and the laws of the universe. —NEIL FIORE, *Awaken Your Strongest Self*

Change Your Name and Succeed

Our ski racing team gathered at Whistler Mountain in Canada's British Columbia to train for the upcoming ski season. Most of us were stuck, as I was, in intermediate level skiing and in need of advanced, expert skills. The day before our lesson on the expert, triple black diamond slope, I thought I'd better examine this infamous hill on my own. It was so steep, so icy, and so cold that I decided that my best hope of surviving was to ski across the slope and take a strategic fall at the tree line on my right. Then, still shaking in my boots, I skied across the slope in the opposite direction, taking two more strategic falls until I was down the most terrifying part of this monster mountain. I made it down the hill without breaking any bones but without much self-respect. I had no idea how I would make it through the next day's expert ski lesson on Blackcomb Glacier.

Luckily, the next day we had an outstanding ski instructor named Wendell. His task was to teach us how to ski the expert black diamond slopes of Whistler and Blackcomb mountains. Wendell took us on a couple of manageable runs and looked over his class of older, anxious hopefuls and said: "You have the latest equipment that allows you to ski effortlessly, but you're struggling as if you still have those old heavy boots and skis from over twenty years ago."

I started taking notes! This was an excellent metaphor for what I see my therapy clients doing when they're trying to struggle with current issues using the limited coping skills of their childhood. When under pressure or distress, we all tend to revert to primitive defenses, forgetting our adult knowledge and strength and losing sight of the opportunities right in front of us today.

As remarkable as Wendell's first statement was, his next remark nearly knocked me out of my skis. He said: "I haven't got time to teach the *old you* how to ski like an expert, so I'm going to change your names to those of native-born skiers." Pointing to one each of us in turn, starting with the women, he called out: "You can be Ingrid, you'll be Heidi." Then the men: "You're Fritz; Franz; Helmut; Hans; Wolfgang; and Neil, you're Jean-Claude Killy."

Stop Waiting for Your Old Identity to Feel Confident

By changing my name and giving me a new identity, Wendell helped me to stop waiting for my old identity to feel confident enough to ski down a formidable glacier. Only my new, Olympic self could ski directly down an expert black diamond slope faster and steeper than I had ever skied. My old self (and name) didn't know how to do it. To ski down this expert slope, I would need to stop the self-doubts of my old identity and its stunted level of confidence. I would have to assume the identity of an expert by getting into the zone far beyond my old, limited identity.

As I slid off the top of that glacier, my old identity was still there, whispering in my ear, "Where are we going to fall? I don't know how to do this." I had to push aside that voice of doubt and fully engage in the thrill of skiing effortlessly, out of my head—with a level of skill only my body knew—down the glacier, faster, straighter, and steeper than I had ever skied before. I saw my skis move back and forth under my body as if in slow motion. I knew I was in the zone—that state in which you perform far beyond your conscious ability. I had seen films of experts skiing in tight S-patterns straight down the face of a mountain, and I knew that's exactly what I was doing without quite knowing how I was doing it. That day there was no need of strategic falls, only perfect harmony with the mountain and the snow. What a thrill!

Wendell's amazing strategy has also helped enhance the power of my coaching with clients. Now when I see how clients are struggling from an old, limited sense of self—an old, outdated identity—I tell them to stop waiting to feel confident. I know their old patterns are keeping them stuck, just as I was stuck skiing at the intermediate level until I learned how to shift my identity to that of an expert skier—an Olympic champion. I now know it's possible for them to quickly access skills and knowledge by letting go of their old identity and opening to their hidden, deeper capability.

How to Conduct a Committee Meeting with Yourself

As we become more able to define our lives, and control our processes in a positive inclusive way, we become like the conductor, allowing each individual member to play a part, and working towards orchestrating the personality into a harmonious whole. This conductor is the self or "I."

—WILL PARFITT, *The Elements of Psychosynthesis*

To take charge of your life, you need to gain the cooperation and contribution of all parts of yourself to create the grander whole of who you truly are. By calling a "committee meeting," you eliminate self-sabotage, resistance, and worry while maximizing your chances of achieving your goals and attaining inner peace.

Playing the role of an orchestra conductor or committee chairperson will enable you to integrate all parts of your personality into a harmonious team, thus avoiding overidentification with any single part of you. In an integrated team approach to taking charge of your life, the leadership Self takes full responsibility for the final decisions, especially when something unexpected or painful occurs.

Resistance and self-sabotage are minimized, because the participation and commitment of every member of the committee is called for before any action is taken. With a shared vision, the cooperation of every team member is more likely. When the Self takes responsibility for the risks involved in any decision, the lesser parts can relax their fears and their tendency to be overly worried about mistakes and losing the approval of authority figures. As you show up more frequently in the role of leader or chairperson, you activate your higher, human brain (what neurologists call the *prefrontal cortex executive function*) and its ability to make choices, weigh pros and cons, make risk-benefit analyses, and assert a clear vision of your goals and values.

It's a "Come as You Truly Are" Party

A number of biologists now suspect that a robustly articulated sense of self . . . is very much the point of the human brain. They propose that consciousness allows humans to manipulate the most important resource of all—themselves—and to use the invented self as a tool to advance their own interests among their peers.

—Natalie Angier, *The New York Times*

Holding a committee meeting with the various parts of you can resolve inner conflict, indecisiveness, and worry in less than a few minutes. What makes these meetings more powerful and more effective than our usual inner dialogue is that you, as the Self, are conducting the meeting in the role of a chairperson. You get to state your vision and objectives and then invite all parts to state their concerns and what they need in order to cooperate and contribute fully. Once objections and

---

An Invitation. All parts are encouraged to attend.

Your Self is having a party. It's a potluck. So prepare your specialty and bring along the perspective of each of your inner voices, their passions, and concerns. Bring your worries—especially the "What if?" and the "Yes, but what if we fail?" voices—as well as your enthusiasm, your energy, and your deep longing to be part of a larger purpose. Be ready to answer with "This is what I will do if."

concerns about past failures and hurts are addressed, support for the Self's leadership vision is garnered. In order to create an integrated team effort, cooperation must replace inner conflict and commitment must replace compliance.

Conducting a Committee Meeting

Step 1. Sit comfortably with your eyes closed and look inward. Visualize a boardroom or meeting in which you are in the chairperson's seat and role. Take at least three breaths to float down into the support of the chair and to let go of muscle tension.

Step 2. State your goals, vision, and mission to all assembled and invite their cooperation and contribution. For example: "I want to lose twenty pounds. I'm committed to making exercise a regular part of my week. I'm committed to protecting my body from its addictive habits. I'm no longer using food as a drug or a solution to all problems. Food and eating will no longer occupy my mind as if they're the answer to everything. I want your cooperation."

Step 3. Invite all parts to express their cooperation, resistance, or concerns. (As with any meeting, you can expect some members to say, "We tried that before, and it didn't work" or, "What if it backfires like last time, and you gain weight, get depressed, hate yourself, and make all of us miserable?")

Step 4. Answer all "What if's" with the "Yes . . . and" template."

Yes, it would be very upsetting if that happened.

Yes, it would hurt.

Yes, that would be awful.

And I would choose to accept and forgive myself, get help, and start again. If that happens, I will not let it ruin our weekend. I have a plan for bouncing back.

And my overall plan is, *regardless of what happens, I will not make you feel bad.*

Step 5. Ask: "What do you need to hear from me in order to fully cooperate and participate in achieving this goal?" (The usual responses require you, the Self, to act as a leader who provides safety, acts from choice, protects every part from criticism, and has a plan to recover from disappointment and setbacks.)

Once the chairperson provides the five qualities of inner peace—safety, choice, focus, presence, and connection—all parts of you will cooperate and follow your lead after the first committee meeting. It's not unusual to need a few more brief daily meetings to answer all worries and to gain the total cooperation of every part.

With persistent problems, such as procrastination or difficult and worrisome challenges, gather together all the usual suspects—the rebel voice, the dictator, the worrier, the people pleaser, and all fearful parts— each day for a committee meeting of five to ten minutes to reconsider your issues and goals. You'll learn that spending a few minutes integrating all parts of yourself makes it possible to eliminate ambivalence, procrastination, and self-sabotage, thereby allowing you to make considerable progress in achieving your goals. Seemingly immovable blocks can disappear when all parts of you are pulling together in a team effort, and the resultant boost in your energy and motivation can be remarkable.

The Power of the Third Chair Perspective

Another way of stepping into the role of the chairperson or leader of your life is adapted from the Gestalt therapy technique, whereby clients change chairs whenever they take on the voice of a different part of themselves. Placing your various inner voices in different chairs clarifies how inner conflict among the different aspects of your feelings and thoughts keep you stuck.

A client named Peggy could not advance in her career because of her fear of failure on the one hand and her self-criticism and bullying on the other. She was stuck in a tug-of-war between a fearful voice and a tough, bullying voice, each requiring its own chair. Peggy took on the perspective of each side of the inner conflict while I wrote down the voices of each part. I realized that from my third perspective I could see both sides as well as what Peggy wanted to achieve.

I then asked Peggy to take my therapist's chair to gain a new perspective. As Peggy sat in my chair, I shifted between the seats of the other voices and read back what she had said when she had taken on their voices and perspectives. This adjustment to the Gestalt technique brought about an unexpectedly rapid and positive shift in Peggy's attitude and confidence level.

Sitting in the therapist's chair, Peggy easily assumed the role of a confident, compassionate chairperson and leader. From this third perspective, she could hear both conflicting voices and realize what they were doing to her life. Once outside their smaller view, Peggy could be more objective, see alternatives, and remember her commitment to *her* goals rather than their fears and squabbling.

Without exception, every client who has shifted to the third chair perspective and assumed a leadership role has changed their physical posture and voice and, in effect, said to the other parts of themselves: "You guys have been ruining my life. I need you to cooperate with *my* goals. I'm tired of being stuck in the same old self-defeating rut. Now I'm in charge."

As Peggy continued to take adult responsibility for facing her fears and her frightened voices, she "lowered their volume," as she said, making it possible for her to achieve her dream of completing college and advancing her career.

This third chair technique, though discovered thirty-five years ago, retains the essential shift into the third voice of a wise, strong, larger Self that is capable of breaking the tug-of-war between conflicted inner voices. In Peggy's case, it was noteworthy that the third chair was a therapist's chair, representing a role that acts as an accepting and compassionate container for all parts of ourselves and all aspects of the human drama with its sorrows, joys, and potential. By changing her chair, and thus her point of view and role, Peggy was no longer pulled into one part of herself doing battle against another part. She had become unstuck and was free to act from the third perspective of her mature Self. From that perspective, she was able to offer every part of her nonjudgmental acceptance and a leader's guidance.

Exercising Belief in Your Whole Self

What could you do if you weren't stuck in the limited identity and sense of self you've been hypnotized into believing is all that you are?

What if you could expand your identity to include every member of your inner committee: the genius of your subconscious mind, the creativity of the right hemisphere of your brain, and the wisdom of your autonomic nervous system?

Ask yourself, "What would I do if I believed:"*

I could not fail.

_____

I am brave.

_____

I am worthy.

_____

I am confident.

_____

I am creative.

_____

I am lovable.

_____

I can be successful and still be at peace with myself.

_____

* Adapted from "If I Were Brave," an inspirational song by Jana Stanfield.

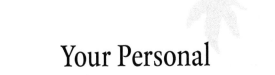

Your Personal Commitment to Action

What is the one task you must be working on today that will give you a sense of deep accomplishment? Focus on getting *started* on the project—even if it's just for fifteen or thirty minutes—that will make a real difference in your life.

_____

When will you choose to start work on your project program? (Specify the day and the hour, for example, 2 p.m. today or 8:30 a.m. tomorrow.)

_____

What part of the task will you start on? (For example, make an outline of key projects; choose to start on one that is the most difficult.)

_____

Which personal priorities do these actions relate to? (Even if the task is boring, you can learn to work with less stress and more creativity and be better prepared for your future job.)

_____

_____

What are your personal deadlines? How will you take ownership of your deadlines? Take the deadlines and create a 3-D picture. Back-time from that future date to when you can start now; include your holidays and deadlines; and divide the project into manageable chunks that are doable in five to ten hours per week.

_____

_____

From whom can you get feedback and support? (Avoid wasting time with perfectionism by asking for feedback early and often.)

_____

_____

How will you delegate low priorities, avoid distractions, and focus? (Take thirty seconds to rehearse and preprogram your commitment.)

_____

_____

Tools: Frequent Phrases to Keep Handy

Here are ten phrases I frequently offer my clients. Some clients paste one or more on their computer or refrigerator. You may find them helpful.

1. You are not the problem, the enemy, or the solution.
2. Ask yourself: *When* can I start?
3. Don't make it a problem.
4. Start your conversation with "Yes . . . and . . ."
5. You will go from not knowing to knowing. Soon you will know something you don't know yet.
6. There is more to you than just your conscious ego.
7. Use your "night shift" dreaming mind to start working while *you* go to sleep.
8. What do *you* want to say to that part of you that says, "I'm afraid? I lack confidence. I don't know what to do. I don't want to."

9. You don't have to *want* to. Human beings can *choose* how to act.

10. Stop asking "Why?" It's a fact. Ask, "What can I do now?"

Bibliography

Bandura, A. (1997). *Self-efficacy: The Exercise of Control.* New York: W. H. Freeman.

Baum, K., and R. Trubo. (1999). *The Mental Edge: Maximize Your Sports Potential with the Mind/Body Connection.* New York: Perigee.

Bly, Robert. (1990). *Iron John: A Book about Men.* Reading, MA: Addison-Wesley.

Bowlby, John. (1969). *Attachment and Loss*, volume 1. New York: Basic Books.

———. (1961). "The Process of Mourning." *The International Journal of Psycho-Analysis* 42:317–40.

———. (1973). *Separation: Anxiety and Anger.* New York: Basic Books.

Carter, R. (1998). *Mapping the Mind.* Berkeley: University of California Press.

Epstein, M. (1988). "The Deconstruction of the Self: Ego and 'Egolessness' in Buddhist Insight Meditation." In *Journal of Transpersonal Psychology* 20, no. 1, 61–70.

Fiore, Neil (1979). "Fighting Cancer—One Patient's Perspective." *The New England Journal of Medicine*, 300:284–9.

Fiore, Neil (2007). *Awaken Your Strongest Self: Break Free of Stress, Inner Conflict, and Self-Sabotage.* New York: McGraw-Hill.

———. (2007). *The Now Habit: Conquering Procrastination with Guilt-Free Play.* New York: Tarcher/Putnam.

Frankl, Viktor E. (1959, 2006). *Man's Search for Meaning.* Boston: Beacon Press.

Goldberg, E. (2001). *The Executive Brain: Frontal Lobes and the Civilized Mind.* Oxford: Oxford University Press.

Helminski, K. E. (1992). *Living Presence: A Sufi Way of Mindfulness and The Essential Self.* New York: Putnam.

Kouzes, James M., Barry Z. Posner, and Tom Peters. (1996). *The Leadership Challenge: How to Keep Getting Extraordinary Things Done in Organizations.* San Francisco: Jossey-Bass.

Lazarus, R., and S. Folkman. (1984). *Stress, Appraisal, and Coping.* New York: McGraw-Hill.

Palmer, Wendy. (2002). *The Practice of Freedom: Aikido Principles as a Spiritual Practice.* Berkeley: Rodmell Press.

Pennebaker, J. W. (1997). *Opening Up: The Healing Power of Expressing Emotions.* New York: Guilford Publications.

Phillips, Maggie, and Claire Frederick. (1995). *Healing the Divided Self: Clinical and Ericksonian Hypnotherapy for Post-traumatic and Dissociative Conditions.* New York : Norton.

Raft, David, and Jeffry Andresen. (1986). "Transformations in Self-Understanding after Near-Death Experiences." *Contemporary Psychoanalysis* 22 (July 1986): 319–46.

Richo, David. (1991). *How to Be an Adult: A Handbook on Psychological and Spiritual Integration.* Mahwah, NJ: Paulist Press.

Sarason, I. G., B. S. Sarason, and G. R. Pierce. (1990). "Anxiety, Cognitive Interference, and Performance: Communication, Cognition, and Anxiety." *Journal of Social and Behaviour and Personality* 5, 1–18.

Seligman, M. E. P. (2002). *Authentic Happiness: Using the New Positive Psychology to Realize Your Potential for Lasting Fulfillment.* New York: Free Press.

Schwarzer, R., and B. Renner. (2000). "Social-cognitive Predictors of Health Behavior: Action, Self-efficacy and Coping Self-efficacy." *Health Psychology* 19, no. 5, 487–95.

Sperry, R. (1982). "Some Effects of Disconnecting the Cerebral Hemispheres." *Science* 217: 1223–26.

Spiegel, H., and D. Spiegel. (1978). *Trance and Treatment: Clinical Uses of Hypnosis.* New York: Basic Books.

Spielberger, C. D., and P. R. Vagg, eds. (1995). *Test Anxiety: Theory, Assessment, and Treatment.* Washington, D.C.: Taylor and Frances: 3–14.

Suinn, R. M. (1993). "Imagery." In R. Singer, M. Murphy, and L. Tennant, eds. *Handbook of Research on Sport Psychology.* New York: Macmillan, 492–510.

Tolle, Eckhart. (1999). *The Power of Now: A Guide to Spiritual Enlightenment.* Novato, CA: New World Library.

Watkins, J. G., and H. Watkins. (1997). *Ego States: Theory and Therapy.* New York: Norton.